TIME TO MOVE

COMPLETE JUNIOR CYCLE PE

DOIREANN NÍ MHUIMHNEACHÁIN
& CONCHÚR Ó MUIMHNEACHÁIN

GILL EDUCATION

Gill Education
Hume Avenue
Park West
Dublin 12
www.gilleducation.ie

Gill Education is an imprint of M.H. Gill & Co.

© Doireann Ní Mhuimhneacháin and Conchúr Ó Muimhneacháin 2020

ISBN: 978-0-7171-88185

Design: Design Image
Illustrations: Katie Gabriel Allen, Derry Dillon and Andriy Yankovskyy

At the time of going to press, all web addresses were active and contained information relevant to the topics in this book. Gill Education does not, however, accept responsibility for the content or views contained on these websites. Content, views and addresses may change beyond the publisher or author's control. Students should always be supervised when reviewing websites.

For permission to reproduce photographs, the authors and publisher gratefully acknowledge the following:
© Alamy: 164, 179B, 190, 198, 202, 213L, 215L, 287d, 287f, 287g, 287h, 289j, 293TR, 293CL, 293B, 305BL, 306; © Cork Schools Orienteering Association: 250, 252, 254, 268; © Freepik: 300; © Gaelic Athletic Association/Sportsfile: 104; © Getty Images: 24L, 28R, 34L, 201R; © Google Earth: 251; © Inpho: 105, 113TR, 129, 135TL, 135TC, 169, 178CR, 186, 196L, 203; © iStock/Getty Premium: xi, viii, 13, 14TL, 14TR, 14CR, 15, 16, 17L, 17R, 20R, 22C, 24C, 24R, 26TR, 28L, 30L, 30C, 30R, 32L, 34R, 36L, 36R, 49T, 49BR, 50, 54, 64, 71T, 71B, 80, 89, 100, 116, 141, 162, 178CL, 180, 182, 188, 189, 210, 213R, 214BR, 215C, 219TL, 219TC, 219TR, 219BL, 219BC, 219BR, 220, 221, 227, 232, 255, 256, 274, 275BL, 275C, 275TR, 276, 278, 281, 287a, 287b, 287c, 287e, 287i, 292CT, 304, 305BR, 305CR, 308, 315TR; © National Council for Curriculum and Assessment: vii, ix; © Shutterstock: xii, 6, 18, 20C, 22L, 22R, 26TL, 26CL, 26CR, 32R, 70, 83, 106, 113TL, 124, 135TR, 139, 178TL, 178TC, 178TR, 178CC, 179T, 194, 196R, 214BL, 214BC, 228, 245, 272, 275TL, 275BR, 277, 280, 282, 286, 292TL, 292L, 292CB, 292R, 294C, 333; © Sportsfile: 20L, 165, 201L, 310; © Unsplash/Chang Duong: 317TL.

The authors and publisher have made every effort to trace all copyright holders. If, however, any have been inadvertently overlooked, we would be pleased to make the necessary arrangement at the first opportunity.

The paper used in this book is made from the wood pulp of managed forests. For every tree felled, at least one tree is planted, thereby renewing natural resources.

Contents

Introduction

Welcome to Junior Cycle Physical Education (PE)! The focus of this subject is to encourage you to develop a love of movement and to learn about and through it. PE is a subject that puts your health and wellbeing at the centre of the learning experience. Together with your PE teacher, you can also choose to do a Classroom Based Assessment (CBA) in PE.

Each strand in this book is designed in a similar way. Here are the main elements.

Rationale

The reasoning behind each strand is provided to help you relate to the unique contribution and benefits of the strand. It answers the question, 'What's in it for me?'

Learning Outcomes

The learning outcomes identify the most important learning that is to be achieved in the strand. The learning outcomes for each strand are taken from the NCCA Junior Cycle Short Course Specification 2015. When you have achieved the learning outcomes you – or your teacher – can tick them off.

Self/Peer Assessment Tasks

We will look at each learning outcome in turn with activities that are practical and engaging. These tasks will help you to analyse performance and reflect on your progress towards the challenge in hand.

Prior Knowledge

You will be asked to identify your starting point by completing a task. The task establishes a link with your experience and what you already know, and provides the starting point for the journey ahead.

Hot Links

Links to online video clips and resource material are provided. These links provide scope for you to investigate independently and provide you with additional insight into and support on topics that arise in class.

Class Challenge

The class challenge is left blank for the teacher to identify the event/performance/ product that the class will work towards achieving. The challenge may arise from the NCCA-designed Classroom Based Assessment (CBA, 2015), from the 'Rich Task' concept introduced by the Junior Cycle Support Service (2003–2008), or from discussion between you – the students – and the teacher.

My Challenge

Individual challenges provide scope for you to identify and take responsibility for your own improvement. You are asked to identify a personal target for the unit – something you would really like to achieve; for example, in gymnastics it could be: 'I would really like to be able to do a cartwheel.'

PE Passport

This section provides you with a unique profile that is designed for keeping a record of your experiences and your achievements over the course of the three years of Junior Cycle. Take care to keep it up to date.

Indicators of Wellbeing

Tasks that link explicitly to Wellbeing are identified by these icons:

❤	Active
✋	Responsible
🌍	Connected
🌱	Resilient
🤝	Respected
💡	Aware

Key Skills Indicators

These icons indicate Key Skills:

	Being Literate		Being Numerate
	Managing Myself		Being Creative
	Staying Well		Communicating
	Managing Information and Thinking		Working with Others

 Fact file: Interesting facts linked to the unit will be introduced randomly. This information will provide an opportunity for discussion and reflection and ease progression into Senior Cycle.

 I wonder A question or statement is posed to prompt discussion when the opportunity arises, for example 'Is it possible to be fit but not healthy?' This will encourage you to consider your thinking on the topic.

Ongoing Progress Review

Looking at it ☐   Working on it ☐   Nailed it ☐

This is located at the beginning of each strand and asks you to update your progress in relation to the Learning Outcomes linked to that strand. It can be checked or signed by the teacher.

Assessment

Doing an activity without assessment is like finishing a game at half-time – there is no conclusion or result! It is important to gauge your overall progress towards the learning outcomes for each Unit of Learning. An assessment opportunity is provided to help you. Additional support is provided for those of you undertaking a CBA in Physical Education.

Key Skills

As you go through life you will need many skills to handle the various situations that you will find yourself in – mixing with others, communicating your opinion, setting goals and so on. The Department of Education and Skills has identified a number of Key Skills that you should develop in all your subjects. These skills are listed below. Where you see a key skill icon beside a task, be aware that you are also working on developing a key life skill as you work on that task.

Key Skills of Junior Cycle

BEING LITERATE
- Developing my understanding and enjoyment of words and language
- Reading for enjoyment and with critical understanding
- Writing for different purposes
- Expressing ideas clearly and accurately
- Developing my spoken language
- Exploring and creating a variety of texts, including multi-modal texts

MANAGING MYSELF
- Knowing myself
- Making considered decisions
- Setting and achieving personal goals
- Being able to reflect on my own learning
- Using digital technology to manage myself and my learning

COMMUNICATING
- Using language
- Using numbers
- Listening and expressing myself
- Performing and presenting
- Discussing and debating
- Using digital technology to communicate

STAYING WELL
- Being healthy and physically active
- Being social
- Being safe
- Being spiritual
- Being confident
- Being positive about learning
- Being responsible, safe and ethical in using digital technology

WORKING WITH OTHERS
- Developing good relationships and dealing with conflict
- Co-operating
- Respecting difference
- Contributing to making the world a better place
- Learning with others
- Working with others through digital technology

MANAGING INFORMATION & THINKING
- Being curious
- Gathering, recording, organising and evaluating information and data
- Thinking creatively and critically
- Reflecting on and evaluating my learning
- Using digital technology to access, manage and share content

BEING CREATIVE
- Imagining
- Exploring options and alternatives
- Implementing ideas and taking action
- Learning creatively
- Stimulating creativity using digital technology

BEING NUMERATE
- Expressing ideas mathematically
- Estimating, predicting and calculating
- Developing a positive disposition towards investigating, reasoning and problem-solving
- Seeing patterns, trends and relationships
- Gathering, interpreting and representing data
- Using digital technology to develop numeracy skills and understanding

KEY SKILLS

Here is what these Key Skills might look like in action.

Key Skill		Key Skill Element
Being creative		Exploring options and alternatives
Being literate		Expressing ideas clearly
Being numerate		Gathering, interpreting and representing data
Communicating		Listening and expressing myself
Managing information and thinking		Gathering, recording, organising and evaluating information
Managing myself		Setting and achieving personal goals
Staying well		Being healthy, physical and active
Working with others		Co-operating with others

Wellbeing

Your health and wellbeing is of central concern in the PE class. You will have many opportunities to develop attributes that will contribute to your wellbeing. Take these opportunities and see how you grow.

INDICATORS OF WELLBEING

ACTIVE
- Am I a confident and skilled participant in physical activity?
- How physically active am I?

RESPONSIBLE
- Do I take action to protect and promote my wellbeing and that of others?
- Do I make healthy eating choices?
- Do I know where my safety is at risk and do I make right choices?

CONNECTED
- Do I feel connected to my school, my friends, my community and the wider world?
- Do I appreciate that my actions and interactions impact on my own wellbeing and that of others, in local and global contexts?

RESILIENT
- Do I believe that I have the coping skills to deal with life's challenges?
- Do I know where I can go for help?
- Do I believe that with effort I can achieve?

RESPECTED
- Do I feel that I am listened to and valued?
- Do I have positive relationships with my friends, my peers and my teachers?
- Do I show care and respect for others?

AWARE
- Am I aware of my thoughts, feelings and behaviours and can I make sense of them?
- Am I aware of what my personal values are and do I think through my decisions?
- Do I understand what helps me to learn and how I can improve?

What is Physical Education About?

Physical Education is an important subject contributing to your overall education during Junior Cycle.

→ You will be actively involved in experiencing a range of different activities that will excite and challenge you.

→ You will be encouraged to develop your confidence in and commitment to physical activity within and beyond school.

→ You will set goals for yourself to improve your ability and your fitness.

→ Wherever your starting point is, you will be helped to participate safely, competently and fairly.

→ You will think about how sport and physical activity can help you to be healthy and well, both now and in the future.

→ Your class will regularly involve creating, improving, leading, performing and reflecting.

→ You will very often play as part of a team, which will help you recognise that learning to work together and respect other people's effort is a key skill for life.

Physical Education is about learning on the move. This book is designed to support you as you learn.

Best of luck on your journey – enjoy it!

Getting On Together

From the phrases listed below, select the five that in your opinion will contribute to making your class a **safe, enjoyable and positive learning environment for everyone**. There are spaces for you to add your own phrases. With a partner, discuss your selection and come to an agreed list of five. The lists will be gathered and a final list will be made from the majority selection.

1	Give everything a go	6	Include everyone	11	Show gratitude	16	Be active	21	No put-downs
2	Show respect and get respect	7	Be friendly	12	Be disciplined	17	Be ambitious	22	Bully-free zone
3	Accept apologies	8	Be responsible	13	Co-operate	18	Have a say	23	
4	Set goals	9	Persevere	14	Be helpful	19	Have fun	24	
5	Do your best	10	Turn up	15	Shake hands and move on	20	Have patience	25	

Expectations for PE Class

My Top Five	Our Top Five	The Agreed List

I agree that I have a responsibility to abide by the agreed list of expectations for a safe, enjoyable and positive learning environment. I accept that failing to do so will be unacceptable and will have consequences.

Student's Signature:

Date:

How You See Things

You may not be able to change a situation, but you can change how you approach it.

The table below contains a number of common negative expressions. From the list below the table, select a more positive way of approaching each situation and write your answers in the right-hand column. The first one has been done for you.

What can I say to myself?

Instead of ...	Try saying ...
I don't get it.	What am I missing?
It's good enough.	
I'm not as good as others.	
I can't make this any better.	
This is too hard.	
I give up.	
I just can't do this.	
I'm afraid to make a mistake.	

→ What am I missing?

→ I can always improve.

→ This may take time.

→ Mistakes help me to learn.

→ I'll use a different strategy.

→ Is it really my best?

→ I'm going to figure out how to do it.

→ I can't do this yet.

If it is to be –
it's up to me!

PE PASSPORT

My Physical Activity Identity

Introduction

This section documents your experience of Physical Education over your three years of Junior Cycle. We call it your passport because it identifies you and your unique set of skills, knowledge and attitudes. Keep it updated and you will be able to trace your journey.

Name: _____

Date of Birth: _____

My Physical Activity Story

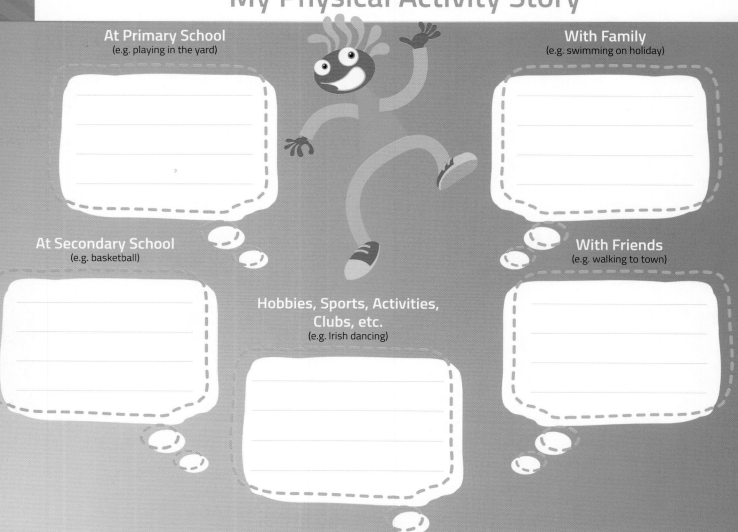

At Primary School
(e.g. playing in the yard)

With Family
(e.g. swimming on holiday)

At Secondary School
(e.g. basketball)

Hobbies, Sports, Activities, Clubs, etc.
(e.g. Irish dancing)

With Friends
(e.g. walking to town)

My physical activity highlights/achievements to date

For example, 'I completed a park run at Ballincollig park on 16 May 2020'.

Why Would I Like to be Physically Active and Fit?

The following is a list of reasons why people might exercise regularly or participate in sport. Add any other reason you feel is missing.

Then list in order of priority (1 = most important) the five reasons that are most important to you.

Relaxation and de-stressing

Fun

Excitement

Competition

1
2
3
4
5

Get fit

Lose weight

Prevent heart disease

Challenge myself

Feel good

Make friends   Look good

Live longer

Sleep well

Refresh my brain

Other: _____

My Sporting Hero

Having someone to admire and look up to is really important.

Name your sporting hero and say what you admire about her/him. There is a space for you to attach a picture below.

These words might help you to explain why you chose your hero.

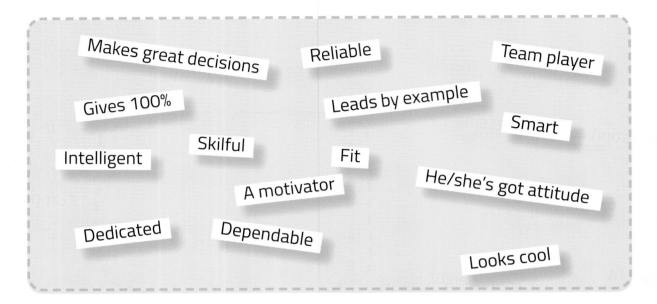

Makes great decisions

Reliable

Team player

Gives 100%

Leads by example

Smart

Intelligent

Skilful

Fit

A motivator

He/she's got attitude

Dedicated

Dependable

Looks cool

My sporting hero is:

Because

If I want to be like my hero, then I will have to:

Attach a picture of your sporting hero

My PE Programme

Use the grid below to map your Physical Education experiences over the three years of Junior Cycle. Any new activity that you spend a number of weeks on is a 'Unit of Learning'. Each time you complete a new unit you can add it to the grid below. Your teacher can help you complete this grid.

Year 1: 20☐☐ - 20☐☐

Unit 1	Unit 2	Unit 3	Unit 4	Unit 5	Unit 6

Year 2: 20☐☐ - 20☐☐

Unit 1	Unit 2	Unit 3	Unit 4	Unit 5	Unit 6

Year 3: 20☐☐ - 20☐☐

Unit 1	Unit 2	Unit 3	Unit 4	Unit 5	Unit 6

Other learning experiences

Clubs/teams/activities I have joined and responsibilities I undertook linked to physical activity in the school.

Year 1: _____

Year 2: _____

Year 3: _____

My Movement Profile

There are a number of fundamental movement skills that form the basis for successful participation in many sports and, in fact, help you to move safely, efficiently and effortlessly throughout your life. Being aware of how you move will contribute to improving your general posture, movement and successful participation in physical activity. In Physical Education, you will be provided with opportunities to assess, refine and develop these key movement skills.

Record your movement skill assessment results here, particularly after the *Fundamental Movement Skills* section (pp. 12–38). Revisit this table to update it as necessary. Use the information as a target for your learning or as a personal challenge.

I wonder What is the difference between ability and skill?

My thoughts: _____

_____

_____

Date						

Movement	Beginning	Getting there	Achieved
Balance			
Throwing			
Striking			
Catching			
Stopping			
Lifting			
Kicking			
Running			
Dodging			
Landing			
Jumping			

My movement skills: targets for improvement

For example:

Before the end of First Year I will be able to run 60 metres inside 10 seconds, lifting my knees high and not bringing my arms across in front of my body.

My movement target for improvement	Year 1

My movement target for improvement	Year 2

My movement target for improvement	Year 3

 A *skill* is an athlete's learned ability to choose and perform the right techniques at the right time. The skill will be performed successfully, repeatedly and with ease. An *ability* is something you are born with, e.g. your ABCs (agility, balance and co-ordination).

My Health-Related Fitness Update

It is really important to be aware of your health-related fitness. This section should be completed by you any time your class undertakes a fitness test/review. Keep it up to date and watch out for how and why your scores change.

Aspect	Date and record		
	Year 1	Year 2	Year 3
Resting heart rate (bpm)			
Target training zone (bpm)			
Aerobic capacity			
Cooper test			
Muscular strength			
Hand grip			
Other: _____			
Muscular endurance			
Curl-up			
Other: _____			
Flexibility			
Sit and reach			
Body composition			
BMI			

My Physical Activity Lifestyle Self-assessment

As you conclude your Junior Cycle, review those skills that help you commit to a physically active lifestyle.

→ Read each statement below. Select and mark the score that best indicates whether the statement is: Really true for me; Sort of true for me; or Really not true for me.

→ When you have answered all the statements, use the information in the results section to consider the implications of your ratings.

Date: _____

		Really true for me	Sort of true for me	Really not true for me	Score
1	I regularly assess my health-related fitness.	3	2	1	
2	I regularly monitor and log my current physical activity levels.	3	2	1	
3	I set realistic and achievable fitness and activity goals.	3	2	1	
4	I have planned a personal programme that includes health-related and performance-related components of fitness.	3	2	1	
5	I have the motor skills necessary to perform several physical activities on a regular basis.	3	2	1	
6	I have more positive than negative attitudes about physical activity.	3	2	1	
7	When time is limited or weather is bad, I find a way to do my physical activity.	3	2	1	
8	I can recognise fitness information that is untrue or misinformed.	3	2	1	
9	I know how to get the support of others in achieving my physical activity goals.	3	2	1	
10	I use strategies to help me stick with it, especially after I have been inactive for a while.	3	2	1	
11	I participate in activities that I am not very good at because I am able to enjoy them, even if I don't excel.	3	2	1	
12	I manage my time to ensure that I can regularly participate in physical activity.	3	2	1	

Results		
Rating	**Individual score**	**Total score**
Nailed it	3	30–36
Working on it	2	24–29
Looking at it	1	Less than 24

Source: Adapted from Concepts of Physical Fitness – Active Lifestyles for Wellness, R. Corbin, R Lindsey et al., 2003

9

FUNDAMENTAL MOVEMENT SKILLS

Fundamental Movement Skills

From the moment you are born you begin to move and explore the world around you. Your movements become more refined and controlled as you grow and play. After a while you find it easy to balance your body, move about freely and control objects like balls and racquets. These types of skills are fundamental to being physically active. They are essentially your vocabulary of movement. The greater your vocabulary, the more sentences and stories you can create and perform. Each time you complete a review of your fundamental movement skills, go to page 6 of the *PE Passport* and record your results.

This section looks at exploring how you move when you play. It will help open up a whole range of physical activity and sport options. Better balance will make skateboarding easier; better control of objects will mean the ball goes where you want it to; better movement will make you a dance floor ninja.

Movement skills terminology

Fundamental	Basic; central; essential.
Stability	Maintaining your balance and control while your centre of gravity changes, e.g. when stopping or landing from a jump.
Locomotion	Moving your body position in different ways: walking, running, jumping
Manipulate	Control, manoeuvre or adjust an object, e.g. trapping, kicking or striking a ball.
Co-ordinate	Move or manage two or more things in an organised way.
Force	The energy behind or strength of a movement – light, moderate, strong.
Analyse	Look closely at something to gain insight; study, explore and consider in order to make decisions.
Skill	The learned ability to choose and perform the right technique at the right time, successfully, consistently and with ease.
Technique	The physical movement procedure that is followed in order to perform a skill – it improves with time and practice.
Ability	Something you are born with, e.g. your ABCs – agility, balance, co-ordination.

I wonder Does practice make perfect?

My thoughts:

What are the characteristics of a skilful performer? Think of someone who is very skilful. Glue or draw their picture in the box below.

My chosen performer demonstrates:

_____

_____

_____

_____

_____

Name _____

Go to YouTube and search for 'Two of the World's Best Female Athletes Help Push Each Other to Next Level' (6:25).

In this unit you will assess yourself on a variety of fundamental movement skills.

Balance

The body is held steady by keeping your centre of gravity above your base of support. When you move, jump or skip, your centre of gravity moves and shifts with you.

Try the following activities with a partner, first on your dominant leg and then on your non-dominant leg. What do you notice that helps to give you greater stability? You could record your movement and analyse it afterwards.

1. Move along a low bench, then stop. Standing on your dominant leg, steady your balance and pick up an object from the bench. Continue along the bench to the other end.

2. Repeat while looking at a distant object.

3. Repeat while standing on your non-preferred leg.

My Review

What made balancing easier was:	1 _____
	2 _____
	because ...
	_____
	_____
What made balancing harder was:	1 _____
	2 _____
	because ...
	_____
	_____

Dynamic balance

Surfing involves the ability to maintain a balanced position while moving.

Analyse the position of a surfer, like the one above, and identify what is helping them to maintain their balance.

Head	
Arms	
Legs	

Assessment task

These are some more challenging balancing tasks. Get permission from your teacher before you undertake either challenge. Observe your partner undertake these challenges and complete the observation sheet.

Balance test 1

→ Place four foam tubes on the floor as shown in the illustration.

→ Step from one foam tube to the next without touching the floor.

15

Balance test 2

→ Sit on the balance sphere as shown in the illustration and remain in balance for as long as possible.

Balance test 3: The clock

→ Stand facing your partner, two metres apart.

→ Taking turns, balance on one leg, standing upright, with head up and hands on hips. Visualise a clock and point one arm straight overhead to 12, then to the side at 3, and then circle low and around to 9 without losing your balance.

→ Repeat, standing on the other leg.

→ Make the challenge harder by having your partner call out different times to you.

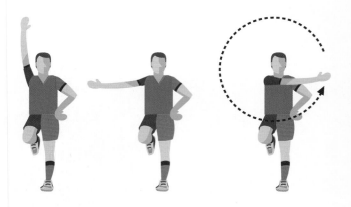

How would you rate your balance? Use the criteria outlined below to make your assessment. Tick the relevant box in each case. Highlight any aspect that needs more work.

Balance Skill Analysis			Date		
	Beginning	**Getting there**	**Achieved**	**Needs work**
Balance is stable on both legs				
Head up, eyes focused				
Re-balancing is prompt				

Throwing

What do you know about how to throw?

Why should you learn how to throw?

Where do you aim when throwing to someone?

Play the following game. Your aim is to identify what makes a good overarm throwing technique. Pay particular attention to your arms and stepping action.

Numbers game

→ For each grid there are four players, numbered 1–4.

→ Players throw a tennis ball **overarm** to each other in numbered order (1–2–3–4) while walking round the grid.

→ Now throw in reverse order (4–3–2–1).

→ Repeat the same process (1–2–3–4; 4–3–2–1) while jogging, then skipping, then hopping.

→ Change to an **underarm** throw. Repeat the same process (1–2–3–4; 4–3–2–1; walking, jogging, skipping, hopping).

Change it

→ Your teacher will call a number. That number player swaps with the same number player from another grid.

→ The selected number is 'piggy in the middle'.

→ Each time a player intercepts the ball they win a point for their original team.

My Review

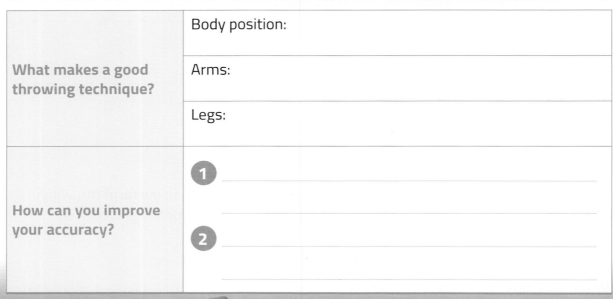

What makes a good throwing technique?	Body position:
	Arms:
	Legs:
How can you improve your accuracy?	1 _____
	2 _____

Assessment task

With a partner, try these two activities and analyse your partner's performance using the criteria that follow. You could record the throwing performance and review it afterwards.

Throw 1: Quick throw

→ With your partner, throw and catch a tennis ball without hesitation for 1 minute without stopping.

→ Work on framing and quick release.

Throw 2: Throwing from a distance

→ With your partner, throw and catch a tennis ball, gradually moving further apart.

→ Throw *directly* to the receiver.

→ No lob throws.

→ This builds valuable arm strength.

How would you rate your throwing? Use the criteria outlined below to make your assessment. Tick the relevant box in each case. Highlight any aspect that needs more work.

Throwing Skill Analysis Date ☐☐ ☐☐ ☐☐	**Beginning**	**Getting there**	**Achieved**	**Needs work**
Body side on opposite arm points to target				
Ball thrown with wrist action				
Follow-through across body in downward arc				
Weight transferred forward to leg on non-throwing side				

Striking

Play the following game. Try to identify what makes a good striking technique. Then answer the review questions that follow. Pay particular attention to your body position, arms and stepping action.

Call and target

Equipment: tennis ball; bat; two markers for bases – pitching and batting; three pairs of cones of different colours (e.g. two green, two red, two yellow).

Playing area: 15 m x 8 m. Distance from pitching base to batting base: 7 m.

The game:

→ Two teams of four.

→ Player Z identifies one mini-goal as the target for the batter.

→ Player Y pitches the ball to player X (the batter) to strike. The ball must not be pitched above the batter's shoulder or below their knee.

→ The batter aims to place the ball in the designated mini-goal.

→ Each batter receives five pitches.

→ The backstop or a fielder returns the ball to the pitcher.

My Review

What is the best way to hold the bat?	
How do you make sure you strike the ball?	
How did you improve your accuracy?	

Assessment task

In groups of four, play the game below and analyse your partner's performance using the criteria that follow. You could record the striking performance and review it afterwards. Highlight any aspect that needs more work.

Target practice

Equipment: tennis ball; bat; wall target; two markers for bases – pitching and batting.

Playing area: Distance from pitching base to batting base: 7 m.

The game:

→ The batter aims to strike the target with the ball.

→ Each player has five turns: two balls self-feed; three balls from the pitcher.

→ The ball must not be pitched above the batter's shoulder or below their knee.

→ Fielder returns the ball to the pitcher.

→ One team member acts as recorder/observer.

How would you rate your striking? Use the criteria outlined below to make your assessment. Tick the relevant box in each case. Highlight any aspect that needs more work.

Striking Skill Analysis   Date ☐☐ ☐☐ ☐☐

	Beginning	Getting there	Achieved	Needs work
Body side-on to the throw				
Eyes on the ball				
Fluid movement as weight transferred from back leg to front				
Ball struck with full arm extension				
Follow-through across the body				

Catching

Play the following game. Your aim is to identify a good catching technique. Then answer the review questions that follow. Pay particular attention to your body position, eyes and arm action.

Across the line

Equipment: Basketball.

Playing area: Catching and throwing lines 10–15 m apart.

The game:

→ Two teams of eight (or more) players each.

→ One team splits into two and stands on the throwing lines, four players on either side. They throw the ball over the middle zone to their teammates, who catch it on the other side. The ball can be passed up and down the throwing line. A point is scored for each successful catch.

→ The team in the middle zone try to intercept the ball.

→ Teams change over when three throws have been intercepted.

→ Play is continuous.

→ Middle zone players must remain 1 m from the throwers.

My Review

What must you do with your feet?	
How long do your eyes stay on the ball?	
What is the best way to catch the ball?	
What does the term 'soft hands' mean?	

Assessment task

In a group of three, play the following game and analyse your partners' performance using the criteria that follow. You could record the catching performance using HUDL or Coach's Eye and review it afterwards. Make a note of any aspects that need attention.

High catch

→ One thrower, one catcher and one observer.

→ The thrower begins with an underarm throw from 5 m.

→ The catcher aims to field the ball above their head.

→ After each successful catch, the catcher steps back 2 m.

→ The observer analyses the catcher's technique.

How would you rate your catching? Use the criteria outlined below to make your assessment. Tick the relevant box in each case. Highlight any aspect that needs more work.

Catching Skill Analysis

Date ☐☐ ☐☐ ☐☐

	Beginning	Getting there	Achieved	Needs work
Eyes follow the flight of the ball				
Body positioned in line with ball				
Hands/arms soft, absorbing force of ball				
Fingers spread and relaxed				
Timing of catch is effective				

Stopping

The skill of quickly slowing down (deceleration) is important in many sports. 'It's no good having the speed of a Ferrari if you have the brakes of a Yugo.'

Play the following game. The aim is to identify what makes a good stopping technique. Answer the review questions that follow. Pay particular attention to your body position, arms and leg action. Recorded analysis would be very helpful to observe the movement in slow motion.

Mirror

→ Two players face each other on either side of a mid-line.

→ The player with the ball can move in any direction within their 5 m x 5 m zone.

→ The opposing player must mirror every move of the player with the ball, for example if the ball carrier moves forward, the opposing player reverses in the same direction.

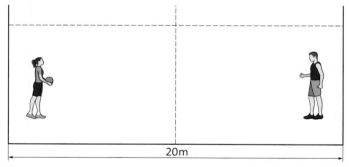

20m

My Review

Which movements were most difficult to mirror as a defender?	
How did you stop and change direction quickly?	
How did you keep your balance?	

Assessment task

In a group of three, try the following activity and analyse the performance using the criteria that follow. You could record it (e.g. using HUDL or Coach's Eye) and review it afterwards. Highlight any aspect needing attention.

Run in

→ Two players begin 20 m apart. A is the attacker and B is the defender.

→ They sprint towards each other (towards the red cone).

→ They stop close to the red cone. Whichever direction A moves, B has to shadow.

→ The third player observes and analyses.

→ Then swap roles.

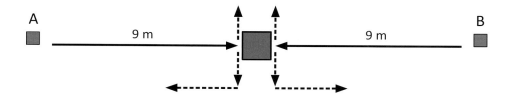

How would you rate your stopping? Use the criteria outlined below to make your assessment. Tick the relevant box in each case. Highlight any aspect that needs more work.

Stopping Skill Analysis Date	Beginning	Getting there	Achieved	Needs work
Stopping is controlled and immediate				
Centre of gravity is low and behind braking step				
Hips, knees and ankles are flexed				
Head is up				

Lifting

The skill of lifting and its contribution to physical activity, sport and daily life is often overlooked. A safe lifting technique reduces the risk of back injuries.

Go to YouTube and search for 'Proper Lifting Techniques' (3:19).

Team challenge: Tyre tower

Equipment: Five tyres; two posts set 5 m apart.

The challenge:

→ Teams of six members.

→ Each team has a set of five tyres numbered 1–5 placed on a post.

→ The aim is to move all the tyres to the second post within 10 minutes.

→ The tyres must end up in the same 1–5 order.

→ Lift the tyres using the correct lifting technique.

→ You have 3 minutes to consider possible solutions before beginning the challenge.

Rules:

→ Only one tyre may be moved at a time.

→ A tyre can only be placed on top of a tyre with a higher number than it, i.e. tyre 3 can be placed on top of tyre 4 or 5 but not on tyre 1 or 2.

→ Tyres can be moved in any direction.

My Review

How did you make sure that everyone fully understood the challenge?	
If things weren't working out, did you reconsider the plan or muddle through?	
How well did you use your legs when lifting?	
How did you reduce the risk of damaging your back?	

Assessment task
Bench lift challenge

In a group of four, try the following activity and analyse the performance using the criteria that follow.

→ Two team members lift and two observe.

→ The two lifters stand at each end of a gymnastics bench. They bend and lift the bench until they are standing upright.

→ After each lift, place an additional tall cone/marker on the bench.

→ See how many cones you can lift on the bench without any falling off.

How would you rate your lifting? Use the criteria outlined below to make your assessment. Tick the relevant box in each case. Highlight any aspect that needs more work.

Lifting Skill Analysis

Date ☐☐ ☐☐ ☐☐

	Beginning	Getting there	Achieved	Needs work
Stance is wide and stable				
Body positioned close to load				
Head and chest up				
Lift is smooth, using leg muscles				
Load is kept close to body – feet flat on floor				

Kicking

Play the following game with the purpose of identifying what makes a good kicking technique. Pay particular attention to how your body leans and to your stepping action.

Go to YouTube and search for 'UEFA Women's Champions League final - Lyon v Paris - The full penality shoot-out' (3:45).

Cone skittles

This game is played with two teams of five players. Each team has five cones on their goal line. The aim is to kick the ball at the cones to knock them over. You cannot cross over the mid-line and you cannot touch the ball with your hands.

My Review

Who knocked over the most cones?		
What did they do that helped them knock the cones over?	Body position:	
	Arms:	
	Legs:	
How could you improve your kicking?	①	
	②	

Assessment task

On the wall are different posters/stickers. Each poster/sticker is worth a different number of points. Your aim is to reach the number 21 as quickly as possible by hitting the posters/stickers with the ball.

How would you rate your kicking? Use the criteria outlined below to make your assessment. Tick the relevant box in each case. Highlight any aspect that needs more work.

Kicking Skill Analysis	Date				
	Beginning	Getting there	Achieved	Needs work
Eyes on the ball				
Non-kicking foot placed beside the ball				
Long, fast leg swing, coming from the hip				
Strike through the bootlaces or instep				

Running

Play the following game. The aim is to identify what a good running technique looks like. Pay particular attention to keeping your knees high and to your arm and leg action.

Go to YouTube and search for 'Sprint Form Slow Motion' (1:49).

Noughts and crosses

→ One team has Xs (blue cones) and the other has Os (red cones).

→ Players begin from lying on their stomach on the floor.

→ You must run out 15 m to the grid, drop the cone and run back to your team.

→ The first team to get three in a row wins.

My Review

Who was the fastest person on your team?	
What did they do that helped them run so fast?	Body position:
	Arms:
	Legs:
How could you improve your running?	1 _____
	2 _____

Assessment Task
Colour-coded

→ Teams of six. Number yourselves 1–6.

→ Each team starts at the centre line of the hall.

→ Each team has two buckets/containers and four different coloured balls/beanbags, e.g. blue, red, green, yellow.

→ Place one bucket at either end of the hall opposite each team.

→ To begin, place two balls/beanbags in one bucket at one end of the hall and the other two balls in the opposite bucket. (Every team must have the same colours in the same buckets.)

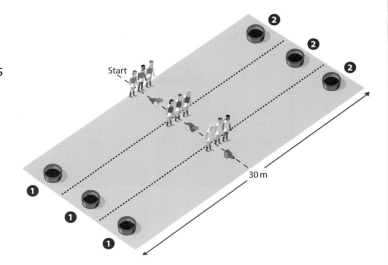

→ Each number races against their matching number (all no. 1s, all no. 2s and so on).

→ The teacher calls 'Go' and a colour, e.g. 'Go blue'. The runners must locate that colour ball/beanbag, take it from the bucket, place it in the other bucket and run back to their team.

→ The first one back is the winner.

→ The game continues with the next number.

How would you rate your running? Use the criteria outlined below to make your assessment. Tick the relevant box in each case. Highlight any aspect that needs more work.

Running Skill Analysis   Date ☐☐ ☐☐ ☐☐

	Beginning	Getting there	Achieved	Needs work
Length of stride is good				
Knees at 90 degrees, kickback is clear				
Rhythm between arms and legs				
Flight phase is evident				
Supporting leg extends fully				
Head is stable				

Dodging

Play the following game. The aim is to identify what makes a good dodging technique. Pay particular attention to the way you lean your body and your centre of gravity.

Take the tag

Go to YouTube and search for 'Best Rugby Steps – Ankle Breakers HD' (10:03).

→ Place a tag in the back of your waistband.

→ The aim is to steal as many tags as possible from other people and add them to those in your waistband.

→ The person with the most tags when the 1-minute time limit runs out wins.

My Review

Who had the most tags in the class?	
What movements helped you avoid having your tag taken?	Body position:
	Arms:
	Legs:
How could you improve your dodging?	1 _____ _____ 2 _____ _____

Assessment task
Me and my shadow

→ Form groups of four.

→ Two members of the group observe and record the others' movement. The other two are 'Me' and 'My Shadow'.

→ Players stand opposite each other, at arm's distance, either side of a court line.

→ On 'Go', Me tries to lose My Shadow before the whistle is blown.

→ Players may only move parallel to court lines.

→ Change positions after the whistle.

→ After two attempts each, swap with the observers.

How would you rate your dodging? Use the criteria outlined below to make your assessment. Tick the relevant box in each case. Highlight any aspect that needs more work.

Dodging Skill Analysis   Date ☐☐ ☐☐ ☐☐

	Beginning	Getting there	Achieved	Needs work
Lean body forwards and bend knees				
Movement in every direction is smooth, quick and co-ordinated				
Centre of gravity is low				

33

Landing

Play the following game and try to identify what makes a good landing technique.
Pay particular attention to how lightly or heavily you land and how you bend your knees.

Go to YouTube and search for 'Box Drop - Landing Mechanics' (0:43).

Shark!

→ Different pieces of equipment will be placed around the hall. These are safe zones. You can only stand on them for five seconds before you have to move.

→ Two sharks – chasers – will be chosen from the class.

→ If you are caught, you join the sharks' team.

→ Be careful when you are jumping on and off equipment:

- Always land on two feet, bend your knees and keep your head up.

- Be aware of people around you.

- Make sure the area is clear before entering or exiting a safety zone.

My Review

Was my landing controlled?	
What was my body doing when I landed?	Body position:
	Arms:
	Legs:
How could I improve my landing?	**1**
	2

Assessment task

You will have a flat cone/tape line beneath you. Your focus will be on trying to land on the cone/tape and on the quality of your landing.

→ Jump as high as you can.

→ Jump and tuck.

→ Jump 180 degrees.

How would you rate your landing? Use the criteria outlined below to make your assessment. Tick the relevant box in each case. Highlight any aspect that needs more work.

Landing Skill Analysis
Date ☐☐ ☐☐ ☐☐

	Beginning	Getting there	Achieved	Needs work
Looking at and focused on the target				
Stable base is clear and wide				
Force is absorbed through ankles, knees and hips by bending				
Landing is safe and controlled				

Jumping

Play the following game. The aim is to identify what makes a good jumping technique. Pay particular attention to how you swing your arms.

Go to YouTube and search for 'Top Broad & Vertical Jumps | 2019 NFL Scouting Combine Highlights' (4:54).

Jump the river

→ Form groups of three. Number yourselves 1, 2, 3.

→ Start at one side of the hall.

→ Player 1 jumps first, as far as they can. Player 2 jumps from wherever player 1 landed. Player 3 jumps from where player 2 landed.

→ Continue to jump in this sequence until you make it across the hall.

→ The team with the fewest number of jumps wins.

Challenge yourself!

See how few jumps you can make to get across the hall.

My Review

Who jumped the furthest in my group?	
What did they do that helped them jump so far?	Body position: Arms: Legs:
How can I improve my jump?	1 _____ 2 _____

Assessment task

→ Place a gymnastics mat on the floor and a mini hurdle across the shorter length of the mat.

→ In turn, jump from standing, over the hurdle and onto the mat.

→ Place a cone or marker on the floor beside the mat to signify where you landed.

→ You get three jumps to travel as far as possible.

→ If you do not land with control you must retake your jump when your turn comes round again.

→ The winner is the person who travels the furthest.

How would you rate your jumping? Use the criteria outlined below to make your assessment. Tick the relevant box in each case. Highlight any aspect that needs more work.

Jumping Skill Analysis

Date ☐☐ ☐☐ ☐☐

	Beginning	Getting there	Achieved	Needs work
Ready position: deep crouch, swinging arms behind				
Forward and upward arm movement when taking off				
Full extension in feet, ankles and knees, in time with arms				
Soft landing, body leaning forwards with control				

STRAND 1

Physical Activity for Health and Wellbeing

Introduction to Physical Activity for Health and Wellbeing

Looking at it ☐   Working on it ☐   Nailed it ☐

This strand of your Physical Education programme will provide you with experiences and knowledge that will help you make choices that contribute to a healthy lifestyle. To achieve a healthy lifestyle and/or improve your performance in physical activity, you need to take care of your **health** and your **fitness** and you need to be regularly **active**. It's your body and your choice, but remember – this body will carry your brain around for the rest of your life. A healthy body is a **pro-brainer**.

The World Health Organisation recommends at least 60 minutes of moderate- to vigorous-intensity physical activity every day to improve cardiorespiratory and muscular fitness, bone health and maintain a healthy body weight. You also feel better … really!

I wonder Is it possible to be fit and not healthy? How?

My thoughts: _____

_____

At the end of this strand I will be able to:

	Learning Outcomes Strand 1: Physical Activity for Health and Wellbeing	Year 1	Year 2	Year 3
1.1	Set SMART improvement goals informed by my health-related and/or performance-related fitness results and advised by norms for my age and sex			
1.2	Apply principles of training within a personalised physical activity programme designed to improve my health-related and/or performance-related fitness, documenting my progress			
1.3	Evaluate my engagement and progress in the programme, providing evidence of progress made and identifying ways I can further develop			
1.4	Use a range of measurement techniques to monitor and analyse physical activity levels across a sustained period of time			
1.5	Identify a range of strategies to support ongoing participation in health-related physical activity			
1.6	Lead physical activities that young people find enjoyable and can undertake to achieve the minimum physical activity recommendations for health			

Class Challenge:

My Personal Challenge:

Strand 1 terminology

RPE	Rate of perceived exertion. A method of rating your own level of intensity during exercise.
Body composition	The proportion of muscle, fat, bone and water in the body.
CBA	Classroom-Based Assessments – selected to evaluate and report on your achievement in Physical Education at Junior Cycle.
Component	Parts or elements that make up a larger unit, e.g. components of fitness.
Programme	A plan that sets out the steps needed to bring about a desired result.
Nutrition	The process of absorbing the nutrients from the food you take in.
Maturity	The state of being fully developed as an adult. Age is not a perfect measure of maturity, as people develop at different rates.
Norms	The accepted standards or ways of behaving or doing things.
Fitness	The attributes you need in order to do what you need to do in everyday life.
Performance	The demonstration of a task.
Protocol	The exact procedure for undertaking a test.
FITT	In order to overload the body, changes can be made to the Frequency, Intensity, Time and Type of exercise/activity.
Cardiovascular endurance	The ability of your heart, blood vessels and lungs to supply oxygen to the working muscles and produce energy for continuous movement.

Why Should I Exercise?

Here are a few reasons why exercise is good for you.

Put a number from 1 (the most important to you) to 12 (the least important to you) in the box under My Choice beside each reason you select.

Can you identify which of these reasons are good for you Mentally (M), Socially (S) or Physically (P)? Put the letter M, S and/or P beside each reason.

Reason	My Choice	M, S and/or P?
Helps you to have a healthy heart and live longer		
Helps you to maintain a healthy body weight		
Helps to build strong bones		
Improves your physical fitness, strength and flexibility		
Tones your body to help you look well		
Improves your mood and mental wellbeing		
Builds your confidence and self-esteem		
Is a great way to meet new people and socialise		
Improves your posture		
Helps you deal with stress, particularly at exam times		
Gives you more energy		
Can you think of anything else?		

Excuse me!

Here are some excuses people use for not exercising. Fill in the blanks to complete the missing words and be prepared to discuss each excuse in class.

I'm afraid I'll get big m _ _ _ _ _ _
I get enough e _ _ _ _ _ _ _ without a fitness programme
Only overweight people n _ _ _ exercise
I don't have any t _ _ _
I might hurt m _ _ _ _ _
I'm afraid p _ _ _ _ _ will laugh at me
No one e _ _ _ does it
I don't like getting all s _ _ _ _ _
My make-up will be r _ _ _ _ _

Health and Hygiene

 'Health is a state of complete physical, mental and social wellbeing and not merely the absence of disease or infirmity.'

You are not completely healthy if any aspect – mental, social or physical – is missing.

Health

Here are some factors in your life that can have an impact on your health.

Put M, S and/or P (Mental, Social and/or Physical) beside each factor to indicate how it can impact on your health.

1
Physical activity and fitness

☐ ☐ ☐

2
Hygiene – cleanliness, avoiding infection

☐ ☐ ☐

3
Nutrition – a balanced diet, good food preparation and handling

☐ ☐ ☐

4
Sleep – good quality and enough

☐ ☐ ☐

5
Stress – anxiety, calm

☐ ☐ ☐

6
Environmental pollution
– water and air

7
Safety
– avoiding risks on the road,
at school, during play

8
Family life
– living in a caring
family group

9
Use and abuse
of substances – tobacco,
drugs, alcohol

10
Sex education
– personal responsibility and
respect, consent, appropriate
relationships

Hygiene

Good personal hygiene habits will keep you clean and healthy, and stop the spread of germs. Feeling clean and healthy helps you feel confident and builds your self-esteem. Poor hygiene can lead to problems like athlete's foot, ingrowing toenails, blisters or verrucas. Here are some elements of hygiene awareness.

When you take part in PE, what hygiene considerations do you need to keep in mind?

Social acceptance – body odour

Showering/bathing

Cleaning surfaces and hands

Washing food

Preventing the spread of germs,
e.g. from sneezing

Wearing fresh and appropriate clothes

Dental care

For good personal hygiene in PE I need to:	
1	
2	
3	
4	
5	

How Muscles Help Me Move and Perform

A muscle is a tough elastic tissue that makes body parts move. Your body is made up of more than 600 muscles, large and small. You don't have to know them all, but it is good to know the names of the main muscle groups. As you grow, your muscles get bigger and help to make the body's shape. Each has an important role to play in helping you make particular movements.

There are two main types of muscle: skeletal muscles and smooth muscles. You also have a cardiac muscle found only in the heart.

 Did you know that muscles can only pull and not push?

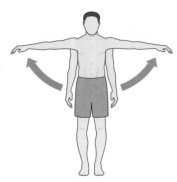

Abduction: When a bone or limb moves *away from* the body.

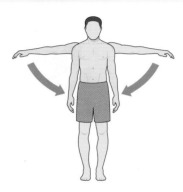

Adduction: When a bone or limb moves *towards* the body.

Flexion: When the angle between two bones *decreases*.

Extension: When the angle between two bones *increases*.

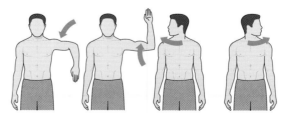

Rotation: When a bone moves *around* a central point in an arc.

Using the image below, connect the muscles to the job they do. The first one has been done for you.

Muscles	What they do	Example
Deltoids	Allow you to stand high on your toes by creating extension at the ankle	Sprinting start
Hamstrings	Create abduction at the shoulder when raising your arm to the side	Swimming arm action
Trapezius	Enables you to flex your trunk	Curl-ups
Gastrocnemius	Allows extension, adduction and abduction at the hip	Jumping, squats
Abdominals	Allow extension of the leg at the knee	Kicking, squats
Biceps	Create adduction at the shoulder across the chest	Press-ups
Latissimus dorsi	Allows flexion of the leg at the knee	Leg action recovery in sprinting
Gluteals	Create extension of the elbow	Throwing, press-ups
Triceps	Allow rotation of the shoulders	Tennis serve
Pectorals	Cause flexion at the elbow	Chin-ups
Quadriceps	Allow adduction at the shoulder behind your back	Rope climb

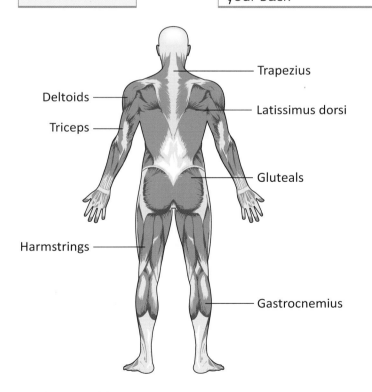

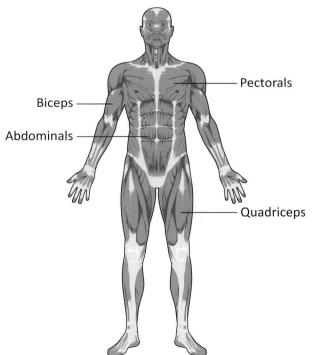

Find out and locate:

What is the largest muscle in the body?	
What is the smallest muscle in the body?	
What is the longest muscle in the body?	

Nutrition: What Does My Body Need?

Your **diet** is the food you eat day to day. It is an important factor in a healthy lifestyle. It's all a question of balance and moderation. A balanced diet is essential for healthy growth and vitality. Health problems arise if we eat too much or too little in relation to the amount of exercise we do. If our energy balance equation isn't right for us, we gain weight or lose weight and we may become overweight or underweight.

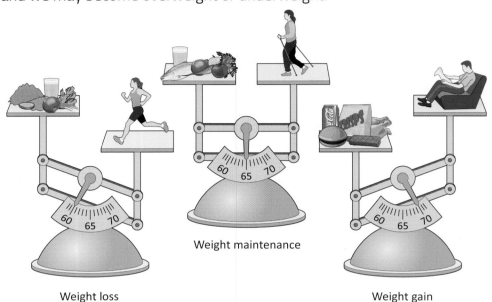

Weight loss   Weight maintenance   Weight gain

There is no 'one size fits all' diet. Your energy needs are influenced by a number of factors. Can you identify what these factors might be?

1	
2	
3	
4	
5	
6	

The food pyramid

The food pyramid is designed to make healthy eating choices easier. Healthy eating is about getting the nutrients you need from the various elements that make up a balanced diet – protein, fat, carbohydrates, vitamins and minerals.

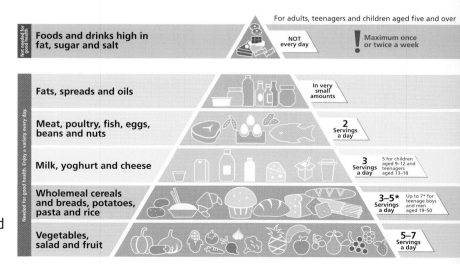

In addition to food, do not forget **hydration**. Drinking plenty of water every day and especially before, during and after exercise is very important.

Below is an Eat Well plate. Based on the food pyramid on page 48, draw a pie chart and label the different types of food that you should include on your plate. Use a bigger slice of the pie chart for the foods you should eat more of, and a smaller slice for the foods you should eat less of.

My Eat Well plate

Get the Most from Your Body

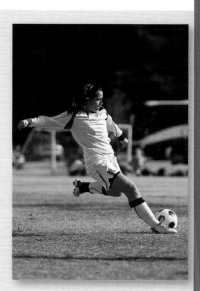

- Never skip meals – especially breakfast.
- Drink plenty of fluids.
- Eat good sources of protein every day.
- Eat lots of carbohydrate foods throughout the day.
- Don't forget fats are important – *choose healthier food sources.*
- Eat at least five portions of fruit and vegetables each day.
- Include good sources of iron and calcium – teens need more of these nutrients than other ages.
- Make sure you enjoy your meals and snacks.
- After intense sport you will be more hungry; don't ignore these hunger signals.
- Get enough rest and sleep – give your body time to grow and recover.

Source: www.safefood.ie

Physical Fitness

> **LO 1.4** Use a range of measurement techniques to monitor and analyse physical activity levels across a sustained period of time.

There are two main types of fitness:

1 **Health-related fitness** is general fitness that enables you to move confidently in your everyday life. When a person is generally fit, they are able to participate safely in physical activity.

2 **Performance-related fitness** is linked to the range of specific fitness components people need in order to deal with the pressures put on their body during sports performance.

Which of these components are health-related and which are performance-related? Fill in the table.

→ Cardiovascular endurance
→ Balance
→ Power

→ Muscular strength
→ Co-ordination
→ Agility
→ Body composition

→ Flexibility
→ Speed
→ Reaction time
→ Muscular endurance

Health-related Fitness	Performance-related Fitness

Components of Fitness
Health-related fitness

Who else strongly needs these components of fitness? Include your example in the boxes below and say why.

Flexibility

Definition: The ability to move joints through a full range of movement.

Example: A person who does martial arts needs flexibility to complete a high kick.

> **Your example:**
>
> _____
>
> _____

Cardiovascular Endurance

Definition: The ability of the heart, circulatory system and lungs to supply oxygen to the muscles for a long period of time without tiring.

Example: A marathon runner needs good cardiovascular fitness to be able to run able to run 42 kilometres (approximately 26 miles and 385 yards).

> **Your example:**
>
> _____
>
> _____

Muscular Strength

Definition: The ability of a muscle or group of muscles to exert maximum force against resistance.

Example: A sumo wrestler needs muscular strength to push his opponent out of the ring.

> **Your example:**
>
> _____
>
> _____

Muscular Endurance

Definition: The ability of a muscle or group of muscles to exert force repeatedly without getting tired.

Example: A tennis player needs muscular endurance to continue returning the ball throughout the match.

Your example:

_____

_____

Performance-related fitness

Who else strongly needs these components of fitness? Include your example in the boxes below and say why.

Agility

Definition: The ability to change direction and speed quickly with control.

Example: A rugby player needs agility to avoid being tackled by an opponent.

Your example:

_____

_____

Balance

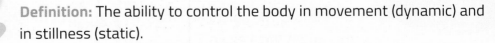

Definition: The ability to control the body in movement (dynamic) and in stillness (static).

Example: A gymnast needs balance when holding a handstand.

Your example:

_____

_____

Co-ordination

Definition: The ability to complete two or more movements simultaneously.

Example: A volleyball player throws the ball to themselves to serve.

> **Your example:**
>
> _____
>
> _____

Power

Definition: The combination of maximum strength and maximum speed in one movement.

Example: A basketball player uses power for an explosive lift off the ground for a slam-dunk.

> **Your example:**
>
> _____
>
> _____

Reaction time

Definition: How quickly a person responds to something such as a ball coming towards them or a gun being fired to start a race.

Example: A goalkeeper moving to stop the ball during a penalty.

> **Your example:**
>
> _____
>
> _____

Speed

Definition: The time it takes to perform an action or cover a certain distance.

Example: A cyclist sprinting to the finishing line.

> **Your example:**
>
> _____

Do you recognise when you use fitness components every day? Rate each of the following activities **high** (H), **medium** (M) or **low** (L) in terms of the cardiovascular endurance, agility, muscular strength and flexibility you need to carry them out.

Physical Activity	Cardiovascular Endurance	Agility	Muscular Endurance	Flexibility
Carrying the shopping				
Tying your shoes				
Carrying your school bag home				
Running for the bus				
Quickly stepping aside to let someone pass				
Skipping				
Walking the dog				
Jogging				
Putting on your socks				
Climbing the stairs				
Sitting with good posture				
Lifting your school bag				
Washing the car				
Digging in the garden				
Reaching for the car seat belt				
Skateboarding				

Create an Activity!

You and your team are now going to create an activity based on one of the components of fitness you just learned about. For example, your component may be cardiovascular endurance and your activity may be a type of chasing game.

Team members:

_____

_____

Our component: _____

	Activity 1	Activity 2
Draw a diagram		
Explain your activity		
Make it harder by …		
Make it easier by …		
Types of sport		
Muscles used		

Fitness Tests

LO 1.4 Use a range of measurement techniques to monitor and analyse physical activity levels across a sustained period of time.

Fitness tests can be used:

→ **Before** you begin a training programme – to assess your level of fitness, discover your strengths and weaknesses to help you create appropriate SMART goals (see p. 80)

→ **During** your programme – to see if you are making progress and to check that the training you're doing is effective

→ **After** you have completed your programme – to see how impactful it was and to check how much you have improved.

These fitness tests will be broken into two sections:

→ Health-related fitness

→ Performance-related fitness.

What influences my results?

There are a number of factors that influence how fit you are or how you perform. Some of these you can change or influence and others you have little or no control over.

Read the list below and tick the factors you can do something about.

Can you think of any other influences? Add them to the list and decide whether or not to tick them.

Smoking		Stress		Physical inactivity	
Genes		Motivation		Weight	
Peer influence		Maturity		Effort	

Now carry out these fitness tests to help you create a detailed fitness profile. Each test is explained, and space is provided for you to record and date your results and compare them to the results for your age group. It is important that you follow the tests exactly as they are explained.

Give it your best shot!

Remember!

These results are where you are at right now. They will help guide you on your fitness journey through setting goals for yourself. **What you do** with this information is the most important thing.

Cardiovascular endurance

Cooper test: 12-minute run

Aim:

- Cover as many metres as possible in 12 minutes.

Equipment:

- Cones
- Measuring tape
- Timer

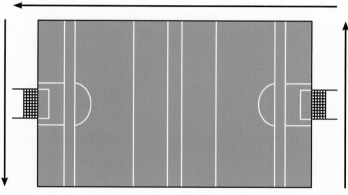

Start/Finish

Method:

- Using cones, lay out a course of a set distance, for example 400 m.
- Run this course for 12 minutes.

12 min

Measurement:

- Calculate the distance you covered.

My Result:

Norms: Cooper test

Rating	Age	
	13–14 years	*15–16 years +*
Excellent	≥2700 m	≥2800 m
Above average	2400–2700 m	2500–2800 m
Average	2200–2399 m	2300–2499 m
Below average	2100–2199 m	2200–2299 m
Poor	≥2100 m	≥2200 m

Muscular strength

Hand grip test

Aim:

- Test the strength of your hand and forearm.

Equipment:

- Grip dynamometer

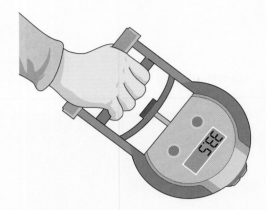

Method:

- Hold the dynamometer in your hand with your elbow bent at a 90-degree angle beside your body.
- Squeeze as hard as you can and then lower your arm slowly to a vertical position alongside your body.

Measurement:

- Take three recordings.

My Results:

Attempt 1	Attempt 2	Attempt 3

Norms: Hand grip test

Rating	Age							
	13 years		14 years		15 years		16 years	
	Male	*Female*	*Male*	*Female*	*Male*	*Female*	*Male*	*Female*
High performance	≥29 kg	≥26 kg	≥36 kg	≥28 kg	≥41 kg	≥28 kg	≤49 kg	≤28 kg
Good fitness	26–28 kg	24–25 kg	32–35 kg	27 kg	37–40 kg	27 kg	45–48 kg	27 kg
Marginal fitness	24–25 kg	23 kg	29–31 kg	25–26 kg	34–26 kg	25–26 kg	42–44 kg	26 kg
Low fitness	≤23 kg	≤22 kg	≤28 kg	≤24 kg	≤33 kg	≤25 kg	≤41 kg	≤25 kg

Muscular endurance

Curl-up test

Aim:

- Test the endurance of your abdominal muscles.

Equipment:

- Timer
- Mat

Method:

- Lie flat on the ground with knees bent at a 45-degree angle.
- Keep your feet apart and put your palms on your quadriceps (thighs).
- Engage your core muscles and reach your palms up your legs until you are in a sitting position.
- Do not lift with your hands behind your head and neck!
- Have a partner hold your ankles so your feet don't come off the ground.
- Do as many curl-ups as possible within 1 minute.

Measurement:

- Count how many curl-ups you can do within 1 minute.

My Result:

Norms: Curl-up test

Rating	Age					
	13 years		14 years		15 years	
	Male	*Female*	*Male*	*Female*	*Male*	*Female*
High performance	≥41	≥33	≥45	≥33	≥48	≥36
Good fitness	21–40	18–32	24–45	18–32	24–47	18–35
Marginal fitness	18–20	15–17	20–23	15–17	20–23	15–17
Low fitness	≥17	≥14	≥19	≥14	≥19	≥14

Flexibility

Sit and reach test

Aim:

● Test the flexibility of your hamstrings and lower back.

Equipment:

● Sit and reach box

Method:

● Take your shoes off for an accurate reading.

● Sit with your legs straight and the soles of your feet flat against the box.

● Place your hands palm down on top of the box.

● Stretch and reach as far as you can.

Measurement:

● Measure the distance you can reach in centimetres.

My Result:

Norms: Sit and reach test

Rating	Age			
	13–14 years		15 years +	
	Male	*Female*	*Male*	*Female*
High performance	≥25 cm	≥30 cm	≥25 cm	≥35.5 cm
Good fitness	20–23 cm	25–28 cm	20–23 cm	30–33 cm
Marginal fitness	15–18 cm	20–23 cm	15–18 cm	25–28 cm
Low fitness	≥13 cm	≥18 cm	≥13 cm	≥23 cm

Body composition
Body mass index (BMI)

Aim:

- To determine how much of your **body** is and isn't **fat**.

Equipment:

- Calculator
- Measuring tape
- Weighing scales

Method:

- Measure your weight in kilograms.
- Measure your height in metres.

Measurement:

- Divide your weight by your height squared. For example, a student who weighs 47 kg and is 1.55 m in height will have a BMI of 19.6, because $47 \div 1.55^2 = 19.6$.

Or:

- Follow our hot link and it will do the calculation for you.

www.bmicalculator.ie

My Result:

Norms: Body mass index (BMI)

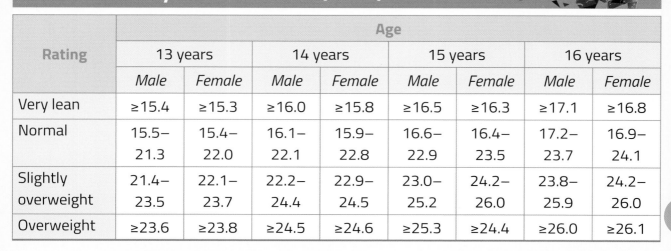

Rating	Age							
	13 years		14 years		15 years		16 years	
	Male	*Female*	*Male*	*Female*	*Male*	*Female*	*Male*	*Female*
Very lean	≥15.4	≥15.3	≥16.0	≥15.8	≥16.5	≥16.3	≥17.1	≥16.8
Normal	15.5–21.3	15.4–22.0	16.1–22.1	15.9–22.8	16.6–22.9	16.4–23.5	17.2–23.7	16.9–24.1
Slightly overweight	21.4–23.5	22.1–23.7	22.2–24.4	22.9–24.5	23.0–25.2	24.2–26.0	23.8–25.9	24.2–26.0
Overweight	≥23.6	≥23.8	≥24.5	≥24.6	≥25.3	≥24.4	≥26.0	≥26.1

Health-related fitness results

Compared with norms for my age and sex.

Test 1 Date ☐☐ ☐☐ ☐☐	My Result	My Rating
Cardiovascular endurance Cooper test: 12-minute run		
Muscular strength Hand grip test		
Muscular endurance Curl-up test		
Flexibility Sit and reach test		
Body composition Body mass index (BMI)		

Test 2 Date ☐☐ ☐☐ ☐☐	My Result	My Rating
Cardiovascular endurance Cooper test: 12-minute run		
Muscular strength Hand grip test		
Muscular endurance Curl-up test		
Flexibility Sit and reach test		
Body composition Body mass index (BMI)		

Agility

Aim:

- Tests your agility by timing how quickly you run and change direction through the course.

Equipment:

- Cones
- Timer
- Measuring tape

Method:

- Lay out the course as shown in the diagram.
- Use the measuring tape to position the cones accurately.
- Lie face down behind the starting line.
- Begin to run when your partner calls 'Go!'
- Time how long it takes to run the course.

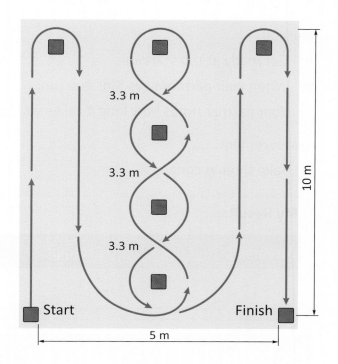

Measurement:

- Take three recordings.

My Results:

Attempt 1	Attempt 2	Attempt 3

Norms: Illinois agility run

	Males	Females
Excellent	≥15.2 s	≥17.0 s
Above average	15.2–16.1 s	17.0–17.9 s
Average	16.2–18.1 s	18.0–21.7 s
Below average	18.2–19.3 s	21.8–23.0 s
Poor	≥19.3 s	≥23.0 s

Speed

Thirty-metre sprint

Aim:

- Tests how quickly you can cover 30 metres.

Equipment:

- Cones
- Timer
- Measuring tape

Method:

- Get ready at the start line.
- When your partner says 'Go!' you run.
- Your partner times how long it takes you to cover 30 metres from start to finish.

Measurement:

- Take three recordings.

My Results:

Attempt 1	Attempt 2	Attempt 3

Norms: Thirty-metre sprint

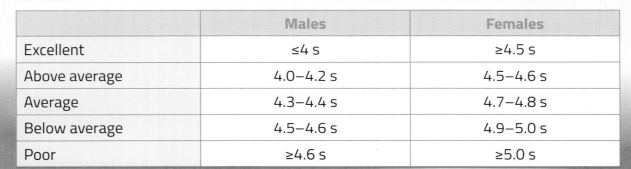

	Males	Females
Excellent	≤4 s	≥4.5 s
Above average	4.0–4.2 s	4.5–4.6 s
Average	4.3–4.4 s	4.7–4.8 s
Below average	4.5–4.6 s	4.9–5.0 s
Poor	≥4.6 s	≥5.0 s

Balance

Standing stork test

Aim:

- Tests your ability to keep your centre of gravity over a foundation of support in a static balance.

Equipment:

- Stopwatch

Method:

- Put your hands on your hips.
- Choose which leg to balance on.
- Place the foot of the other leg against the knee of your standing leg.
- Left your heel from the ground and balance on you toes.
- Your partner starts the stopwatch as soon as your heel has risen from the ground.
- Record how long you can maintain your balance.
- Timing ends if:
  - Your hands leave your hips
  - Your heel touches the ground
  - The foot against your standing leg moves.

Measurement:

- Take three recordings.

My Results:

Attempt 1	Attempt 2	Attempt 3

Norms: Standing stork test

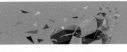

	Males	Females
Excellent	≥50 s	≥27 s
Above average	37–50 s	23–27 s
Average	15–36 s	8–22 s
Below average	5–14 s	3–7 s
Poor	≥5 s	≥3 s

Co-ordination

Alternate wall toss test

Aim:

- Tests hand–eye co-ordination.

Equipment:

- Tennis ball
- Metre stick
- Stopwatch

Method:

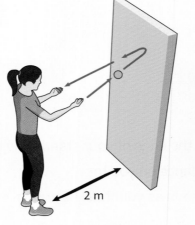 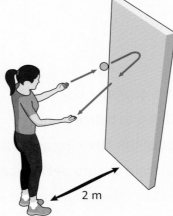

2 m   2 m

- Stand 2 metres from the wall.
- Throw the ball against the wall using an underhand throw.
- Catch the returning ball with your opposite hand.
- Continue in the same way: right-hand throw, left-hand catch, left-hand throw, right-hand catch, etc.
- Your partner will time you for 30 seconds and count how many times you successfully caught the ball.

Measurement:

- Take three recordings.

My Results:

Attempt 1	Attempt 2	Attempt 3

Norms: Alternate wall toss test

	Score (in 30 seconds)
Excellent	≥35
Above average	30–35
Average	20–29
Below average	15–19
Poor	≥15

Reaction time
Ruler drop test

Aim:

- Tests your ability to react quickly.

Equipment:

- Ruler

Method:

- Your partner holds the ruler vertically, holding the top of the ruler.
- Hold your hand with your thumb and forefinger apart at the 0 cm mark.
- Your partner will let go of the ruler.
- Catch the ruler between your thumb and finger as quickly as possible.
- Record the distance it dropped before it was caught.

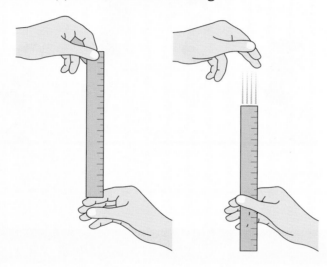

Measurement:

- Take three recordings.

My Results:

Attempt 1	Attempt 2	Attempt 3

Norms: Ruler drop test

Excellent	<7.5 cm
Above average	7.5–15.9 cm
Average	15.9–20.4 cm
Below average	20.4–28 cm
Poor	>26 cm

Power

Standing broad jump

Aim:

- Tests the power your legs can exert.

Equipment:

- Metre stick or measuring tape
- Cones

Method:

- Stand with your toes behind the starting line.
- Bend your knees and hold your arms back.
- Push off both feet and propel your arms forward for momentum.
- Your partner will measure the distance from the start line to where you landed.

Measurement:

- Take three recordings.

My Results:

Attempt 1	Attempt 2	Attempt 3

Norms: Standing broad jump

Rating	Age							
	13 years		14 years		15 years		16 years	
	Male	*Female*	*Male*	*Female*	*Male*	*Female*	*Male*	*Female*
High performance	≥185 cm	≥150 cm	≥203 cm	≥152 cm	≥216 cm	≥155 cm	≥224 cm	≥157 cm
Good fitness	170–184 cm	145–149 cm	185–202 cm	147–151 cm	198–215 cm	150–154 cm	208–223 cm	152–156 cm
Marginal fitness	155–169 cm	136–144 cm	170–184 cm	140–146 cm	185–197 cm	142–149 cm	196–207 cm	145–151 cm
Low fitness	≥154 cm	≥135 cm	≥169 cm	≥139 cm	≥184 cm	≥141 cm	≥195 cm	≥144 cm

Performance-related fitness results

Compared with norms for my age and sex.

Test 1 Date ☐☐ ☐☐ ☐☐	My Result	My Rating
Agility Illinois agility run		
Speed Thirty-metre sprint		
Balance Standing stork test		
Co-ordination Alternate wall toss test		
Reaction time Ruler drop test		
Power Standing broad jump		

Test 2 Date ☐☐ ☐☐ ☐☐	My Result	My Rating
Agility Illinois agility run		
Speed Thirty-metre sprint		
Balance Standing stork test		
Co-ordination Alternate wall toss test		
Reaction time Ruler drop test		
Power Standing broad jump		

Programme Design

> **LO 1.2** Apply principles of training within a personalised physical activity programme designed to improve my health-related and/or performance-related fitness, documenting my progress.

Principles of Training

In order to improve your fitness you need to be organised, disciplined and committed. Planning will be key.

When you are designing a fitness training programme, think **SPORRT**: **S**pecific; **P**rogressive; **O**verload; **R**eversibility; **R**est and recovery; and **T**edium.

→ **Specific:** Marathon runners do mostly long-distance endurance work to match their event.

→ **Progressive:** Intensity gradually increases as the body adapts to the training schedule.

→ **Overload:** You need to make your body work harder, so you need to increase workload. This is achieved by using **FITT** (see below).

→ **Reversibility:** Muscles quickly revert to their original state if training is stopped.

> Use it or lose it!

→ **Rest and recovery:** Exercise can cause fatigue and damage to muscles. Time is needed to recover and ensure safe ongoing exercise.

→ **Tedium:** Training can be boring, and you can lose interest – be aware of the need for variety.

FITT is an easy way to remember how to create extra demands and overload.

F	Frequency	How often you exercise
I	Intensity	How hard you exercise (low/medium/high)
T	Time	How long you exercise for
T	Type	Which exercises are suitable – aerobic, circuit, resistance

Exercise health warning

Before taking on any training programme, do a health risk assessment. Consider:

→ family history

→ prior or existing injuries

→ current medication status

→ health conditions – asthma, diabetes, etc.

→ starting level of physical activity.

Be sensible and work within your limits.

It doesn't have to be hell to be healthy.
'Tóg go bog é ACH tóg é.'

Heart Rate

 Your heart rate (pulse) is the rate at which your heart pumps blood around your body. The heart beats on average 72 times per minute and over 100,000 times in the course of a day. It does a great deal of work.

Resting heart rate is the heart rate taken when the body is rested – normally on waking in the morning before you get up. As soon as you stand up your heart rate changes.

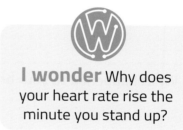

I wonder Why does your heart rate rise the minute you stand up?

Target heart rate is the figure that you want to raise your heart rate to in order to gain the most benefit from exercise.

How to find your heart rate

Taking your pulse in order to get your heart rate takes some practice. Take your pulse for 15 seconds. Multiple this figure by four to convert your score to beats per minute (bpm). Here are two options for taking your pulse.

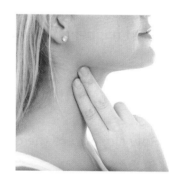

1 **Carotid pulse:** Lightly place the middle and index fingers on the neck, to the side of the windpipe and just below the angle of the jaw.

2 **Radial pulse:** Turn one hand over so that it is palm-side up. Place the same two fingers just below the base of the thumb and between the bone and the tendon.

Which pulse was easier to take – carotid or radial? Why?

_____

_____

Record the Effect of Exercise on Your Body

With a partner, power walk for 15 minutes and run for 7 minutes. Stop after each exercise for 5 minutes' recovery and complete the grid below. Record your heart rate, distance covered, breathing rate (slow, moderate, fast, very fast) and body temperature (cool, warm, hot) in the grid.

Date: □□ □□ □□	Heart rate	Distance covered	Breathing	Body temperature
Power walking				
Running				

What happened to your heart rate? Why?

What happened to your breathing? Why?

What happened to your body temperature? Why?

How close were the distances covered in power walking and running?

Which session did you find harder? Why?

If your heart beats 74 times per minute, how many times would it beat in an hour?

If you had a resting heart rate of 56 beats per minute, how many times would your heart beat in an hour ?

What would be the difference in the number of beats over the course of a day?

What makes your heart muscle stronger?

Getting in the Zone

In order to improve your levels of cardiovascular endurance, you will need to put sensible extra demand on your body. Your heart rate is a good indicator of how much effort you are making. You should aim to get into the target training zone when you train and stay there for a minimum of 10–15 minutes. The upper limit of this training zone is 80% of your maximum heart rate (MHR).

 I wonder Why does the target training zone reduce as you get older?

The formula

To estimate your target zones:

→ Your starting point is always 220.

→ 220 minus your age gives your maximum heart rate (MHR).

→ Calculate 80% of your MHR.

→ Calculate 60% of your MHR.

You now have two HR figures:

→ 80% is the upper limit for your aerobic training.

→ 60% is the lower limit.

Worked example:

Siún is 15 years old.

→ 220 − 15 = 205 (MHR)

→ 80% of 205 is (205 ÷ 100) x 80 = 164

→ 60% of 205 is (205 ÷ 100) x 60 = 123

If Joe's target training zone is between 120 and 160, how old is Joe?

(a) 15 ☐   (b) 2 ☐   (c) 25 ☐   (d) 35 ☐

Calculate the target training zone for each age group.

Age	220 – age	Upper limit (80%)	Lower limit (60%)
14 years			
15 years	205	164	123
16 years			

Estimating your exertion rate
What gear are you in?

You can estimate how hard your heart is working without having to count your pulse rate all the time. You do this using the **rate of perceived exertion (RPE)**. Getting a 'feel for' how hard you are working will help you ensure that you are getting into the target training zone when you exercise.

→ **Moderate activity:** Heart rate is faster than normal and breathing is quicker than normal. (Bottom end of your training zone.)

→ **Vigorous activity:** Heart rate is much faster than normal and breathing is much quicker than normal. (Top end of your training zone.)

The **gears scale** is a JCPE resource based on an adaptation of the Borg scale.

→ 0 = neutral
→ 1st gear = easy
→ 2nd gear = okay (moderate)
→ 3rd gear = hard
→ 4th gear = very hard
→ 5th gear = exhausting

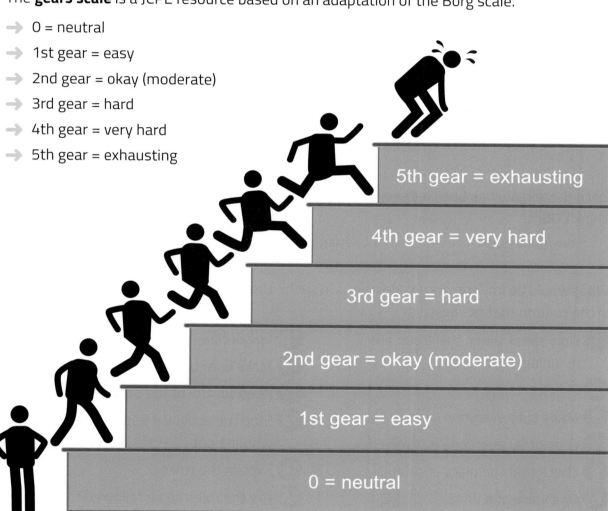

Estimate and record the gear you are working in before, during and after an activity.

Exercise	Rate of perceived exertion (RPE)		
	Before	During	After

Leading a Physical Activity

> **LO 1.6** Lead physical activities that young people find enjoyable and can undertake to achieve the minimum physical activity recommendations for health.

This is an opportunity for you to demonstrate your responsibility and develop your leadership skills. As a member of a group of five, you will each, in turn, lead part of a physical activity for your classmates. The total time duration is 7–10 minutes. Decide on an activity that is not your typical game and which:

→ promotes active participation

→ is not knock-out

→ is inclusive of all abilities

→ helps to practise one or more movement skills.

Once the activity has been agreed, you need to think about HOW you will present it. Think **COG**:

→ **C**ommunication   → **O**bservation   → **G**roup management.

What would be important considerations in each? The following are guidelines. Place them in the column that fits best.

1. Only speak when the group are listening
2. Pick fair teams
3. Make sure everyone can see you
4. Check that everyone is involved
5. Check that the place is safe
6. One voice at a time
7. Is the equipment ready?
8. Keep instructions brief
9. Don't rush
10. Speak clearly
11. Make eye contact
12. Keep control of the ball/equipment
13. Stop the activity if it is unsafe or not working out
14. Explain the rules
15. Are the rules being followed?
16. Apply the rules
17. Ask if anyone has any questions

Communication	Observation	Group management

Now for the Plan!

Group members:

_____

_____

_____

Class: _____   Date: _____

Activity Name:

_____

Movement skills involved:

running ☐   throwing ☐   balancing ☐

jumping ☐   catching ☐   stopping ☐

landing ☐   kicking ☐   lifting ☐

dodging ☐   striking ☐

Other: _____

Brief description (dance, game, challenge, etc.)

_____

Number of members per team/group: _____

Playing area: _____

Main rules:

_____

_____

_____

_____

_____

What happens if rule is broken: _____

Start/re-start rule: _____

Scoring system: _____

Safety considerations: _____

Review

What worked well?

_____

_____

What would make the session better?

_____

_____

What did you learn about good communication?

_____

_____

What advice would you give to another group about working with others?

_____

_____

Which of the following Key Skills elements – *Communicating, Working with others, Managing myself* – did you use? Tick the appropriate boxes.

Communicating	Working with others	Managing myself
☐ Listening and expressing myself	☐ Developing good relationships and dealing with conflict	☐ Knowing myself
☐ Using language	☐ Co-operating	☐ Making considered decisions
☐ Using numbers and data	☐ Respecting difference	☐ Setting and achieving personal goals
☐ Performing and presenting	☐ Contributing to making the world a better place	☐ Being able to reflect on my own learning
☐ Discussing and debating	☐ Learning with others	☐ Using digital technology to manage myself and my learning
☐ Using digital technology to communicate	☐ Working with others through digital technology	

Peer Feedback

This review can be undertaken by a classmate who observed the session and responds to the outline on page 78. Feedback is offered with the intention of supporting each other and should be taken in that spirit. A safe introductory line to your advice would be: 'I liked the way you ...' and 'It would be even better if ...'

What worked well?

_____

_____

_____

What would make the session better?

_____

_____

_____

What did you learn about good communication?

_____

_____

_____

_____

Setting SMART Goals

> **LO 1.1** Set SMART improvement goals informed by my health-related and/or performance-related fitness results and advised by norms for my age and sex.

You are far more likely to achieve your aims if you set yourself **SMART** goals and follow this by planning, recording and monitoring your progress.

Why Bother?

Have you ever tried to hit a moving target? It's much easier if your target stays put! SMART goals set clear targets, help you to focus, increase your motivation, grow your confidence and give a sense of achievement when you make progress. They also help you to plan and measure your improvement.

So what are SMART goals?

Go to YouTube and search for 'Setting SMART Goals – How To Properly Set a Goal (animated)' (6:24).

SMART

- Specific
- Measurable
- Achievable
- Realistic
- Time-bound

Be ambitious – be SMART!

> **I wonder** What if the sergeant said 'Ready, Fire, Aim!'? How effective would that be?

→ **Specific:** Be crystal clear and state exactly what you want to achieve.

TOO VAGUE **SPECIFIC**

→ **Measurable:** A goal is much clearer if you can measure your success or progress against a target. Think time, distance or number.

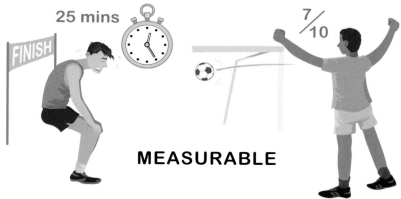

MEASURABLE

→ **Achievable:** Is the goal possible, or is it merely wishful thinking? Consider your starting point. Running a marathon might be your long-term goal, but if you currently run 3 km it is better to start with an achievable 5 km target and progress from there.

ACHIEVABLE

→ **Realistic:** A goal may well be achievable, but consider your access to training resources and the time you have available to train. Is the gym open to students when you are free?

REALISTIC

→ **Time-bound:** Identify a time frame for achieving your goal. There is nothing like a deadline to focus the mind and the effort. You can also tell if you have made progress.

TIME-BOUND

Create a motto for yourself that will inspire you when you need some motivation.

> → *Is fearr rith maith ná drochsheasamh*
>
> → *Every journey – no matter how long – begins with a single step*
>
> → *You miss 100% of the shots you never take*

My motto is:

Strategies to Help Me When the Going Gets Tough

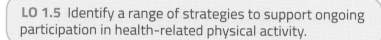

> **LO 1.5** Identify a range of strategies to support ongoing participation in health-related physical activity.

What are My Barriers to Being Active?

The following is a list of reasons why you might not exercise regularly or meet a road block in your efforts to be active.

Number, in order of influence (1 for the most influence; 5 for the least influence), the five greatest barriers to you being physically active. Use the blank squares to add any other reasons you feel are missing.

I'm not bothered		I've no time		Embarrassment		I'm too tired	
I prefer TV/ social media		Friends don't go		I haven't enough money		I have a health issue, e.g. asthma	
Transport – I can't get there		I have too much studying to do		I'm always working			
I'm not the sporty type		My make-up will be ruined		Discomfort – I hate getting sweaty/cold/ wet/dirty			

Check with a partner if they have met similar road blocks.

Can you detour around these road blocks and still reach your destination? How?

Road block	Detour to destination

Here are a few strategies to consider. Select your top five by writing the relevant number (1–5) beside the strategy.

Choose an activity that I really enjoy	
Don't push it too far too early – be aware of how my body feels	
Write it down, post it up and share my goal with friends or family	
Record my progress in a diary/planner	
Always have a way of measuring progress so I know I'm getting fitter	
Reward myself when I reach mini-goals or targets	
Encourage a friend to run with me – an exercise partner	
Power my exercise with great music (note: be aware of traffic!)	
Join a local or after-school club	
Take the dog – do two jobs at the same time!	
Warm up and stretch before any reasonably strenuous exercise – take it easy	
Recognise that I am already resilient – I can do this	
Remember the pay-off – if it's worth doing, it's worth persisting. 'Mam will be sooo proud'; 'I can see myself crossing that finishing line'	
Ask for help	
Other	

Can you tell the class about an occasion when you were at the point of giving up on an activity – at a crossroads – and you managed to come through? What helped you to be resilient?

Like yourself
Count on friends
Adapt to change
Ask for help
Dare to say no

Mental Resilience

Get fit
Go for it
Set goals
Talk about it
Relax and let go
Try something new
Take the bad with the good

My Crossroads Moment

Planning My Personal Physical Activity Programme

> **LO 1.2** Apply principles of training within a personalised physical activity programme.
>
> **LO 1.3** Evaluate my engagement and progress in the programme, providing evidence of progress made and identifying ways I can further develop.

Setting Goals and a Broad Plan

Planning improves your chances of success.

> Failing to prepare is preparing to fail.

Have you ever prepared a written plan to help you achieve your personal physical fitness goals? Here's a little guidance. The following steps will help you get to where you want to be. Qualities like resilience, organisation and self-discipline will be needed for success.

Begin by choosing something that is important to **you** – something that will make you feel, look or be better in your personal fitness. Go n-eirí leat!

Step 1

A Fitness test results.

B Why you want to be fit.

Step 2

→ When are you free to train?

→ Does it require travelling to a gym/pitch?

→ Is there a cost involved?

→ Stickability! Will you stick to the activity?

Step 3

→ Set specific goals that can be measured.

→ Given your situation, are they achievable and realistic?

→ Set a time frame for completing your goals.

Step 4

→ Write down your plan.

→ Put it in your calendar and/or your personal device.

Step 5

→ Is there an app that can help you track your progress?

→ Review your programme midway through and make changes if necessary.

→ Evaluate the overall success of your efforts.

Your mission is to plan for, implement and evaluate a personal physical activity programme over a 4–6-week period. Your programme should be based on results from a recent fitness assessment. Identify at least **two** goals for fitness improvement and review your progress midway. Reflect on your experience and consider how successful your efforts have been.

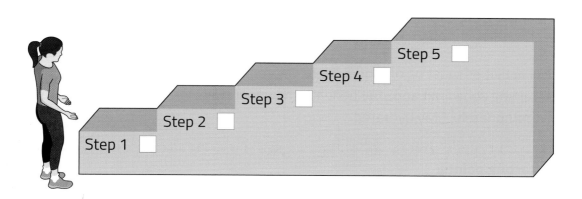

My Personal Physical Fitness Programme

My SMART Goals

1 I want to be able to _____

_____

2 I want to be able to _____

_____

These are important to me because: _____

_____

If I want to achieve these goals, **then** I need to: _____

_____

_____

Target fitness components:

1 _____

_____

2 _____

Physical activities must be of moderate to vigorous level, raise my heart rate above the lower training zone limit and stay beneath the upper training zone limit. Warm up and cool down appropriately. Stay hydrated.

My starting points:

1 I can _____

2 I can _____

My training route:

(Draw a diagram here or print out and stick in a screen grab, e.g. from Google Maps.)

My session plan:

F	Frequency	
I	Intensity	
T	Time	
T	Type	

My weekly plan:

	Monday	Tuesday	Wednesday	Thursday	Friday	Saturday	Sunday
Week 1							
Week 2							
Week 3							
Week 4							
Week 5							
Week 6							

Find some exercise ideas here!

Sworkit Kids

www.fitnessblender.com

My Plan

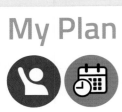

Weeks	☐☐ ☐☐ ☐☐ – ☐☐ ☐☐ ☐☐

Student signature:	
Teacher signature:	

Warm-up

	Activity	Time	Intensity	Notes
Raise HR				
Flexibility				
Movement rehearsal				

Muscular endurance ☐   Muscular strength ☐   Flexibility ☐

Agility ☐   Balance ☐   Co-ordination ☐

Exercises	Sets/Reps	Time	Weight	Rest time	Notes

Cardiovascular endurance ☐   Speed ☐

Type	Distance	Time	Target HR	Intensity	Notes

Cool-down

Exercise	Activity	Time	Intensity	Notes

Mid-term Review (Week 3)

What is my current level (e.g. distance/time/score) and am I on course?

Activity		On course	Off course
Distance			
Time			
Score			

What has helped me to be successful so far?

What changes – if any – do I need to make to my programme plan/approach?

What strategies can I put in place to help me? (Check back to pp. 86–87.)

My Revised Plan

Weeks	☐☐ ☐☐ ☐☐ – ☐☐ ☐☐ ☐☐

Student signature:	
Teacher signature:	

Warm-up

	Activity	Time	Intensity	Notes
Raise HR				
Flexibility				
Movement rehearsal				

Muscular endurance ☐   Muscular strength ☐   Flexibility ☐

Agility ☐   Balance ☐   Co-ordination ☐

Exercises	Sets/Reps	Time	Weight	Rest time	Notes

Cardiovascular endurance ☐   Speed ☐

Type	Distance	Time	Target HR	Intensity	Notes

Cool-down

Exercise	Activity	Time	Intensity	Notes

Conclusion and Reflection

Final Result:

Activity		On course	Off course
Distance			
Time			
Score			

To what degree have I achieved my goals?

In what way was I resilient?

What mistakes did I make that taught me something?

What did I learn about myself and about training?

Physical Fitness Quiz

Review your learning in this strand by circling the correct answer for each question. This quiz can be taken individually or in groups.

1 **Resting heart rate is the heart rate count taken when:**

A   You stop after an intense bout of exercise

B   You are at lunch break and have the time to take the count

C   Before you get up, when you are inactive and relaxed

D   You are inactive and standing up

2 **Which of the following is a measure of muscular strength?**

A   Cooper test: 12-minute run

B   Ruler drop

C   Sit and reach

D   Standing broad jump

3 **Which one of these components of performance-related fitness would a high jumper require as she/he takes off in order to clear the bar?**

A   Agility

B   Power

C   Muscular endurance

D   Reaction time

4 **In the definition of skill, which of the following is not correct?**

A   Learned

B   Genetic

C   Performed with ease

D   Consistent

5 **The average resting heart rate is:**

A   52 bpm

B   102 bpm

C   72 bpm

D   40 bpm

6 During a single day, your heart will beat on average:

A   80,000 times

B   90,000 times

C   100,000 times

D   72,000 times

7 Which of the following is not a wellbeing indicator?

A   Respected

B   Responsible

C   Resilient

D   Resolute

8 SMART is a useful acronym to use when setting your goals. What does the R stand for?

A   Realistic

B   Readable

C   Real

D   Relevant

9 Which of the following statements is true?

A   Regular exercise will guarantee you a healthy life

B   It is possible to be fit but not healthy

C   The higher intensity the exercise, the greater the benefit to your fitness

D   You can be naturally fit and healthy

The CBA

NCCA Assessment Guidelines

For Strand 1: Physical Activity for Health and Wellbeing, students design a Personal Physical Activity Programme.

There are three parts to the Personal Physical Activity Programme:

→ Health-related or performance-related physical activity profile

→ Personal physical activity programme

→ Reflection.

This assessment requires students to plan for, implement and evaluate their personal physical activity programme over a six-week period. During the first two weeks, students will undertake a series of appropriate fitness tests in order to generate a physical fitness profile. In the third week, students will reflect on their results and set goals to improve their fitness levels. Over the remaining three weeks, as students implement their programme, they can be encouraged to reflect on the following: if and how they include regular physical activity in their lifestyles; the kinds of physical activities that they enjoy and are likely to engage in as part of their personal programme; what supports they can use to ensure their success in implementing the programme; and how to address possible barriers to participation that they encounter. On completing this strand, students should reflect on the successes and challenges encountered in implementing their Personal Physical Activity Programme.

Questions such as the following could be used to support student reflection:

→ What went well and why?

→ How would you describe your level of fitness before and after your programme?

→ What didn't go well and why?

→ How did you deal with setbacks?

→ What might you do differently next time?

Assessment features of quality

Exceptional:

→ The programme includes a full and rich profile of the student's physical fitness, addressing the student's personal goals in a realistic way.

→ Well-considered and creative strategies address the challenges in programme participation.

→ The student's reflection is of excellent quality.

Above expectations:

→ The programme includes a very good profile of the student's physical fitness, addressing the student's personal goals in a realistic way.

→ Good, thoughtful strategies address the challenges in programme participation.

→ The student's reflection is of very good quality.

In line with expectations:

→ The programme includes a reasonable profile of the student's physical fitness, addressing the student's personal goals in a realistic way.

→ A range of strategies address the challenges in programme participation.

→ The student's reflection is of reasonable quality.

Yet to meet expectations:

→ The programme includes an inadequate profile of the student's physical fitness, addressing the student's personal goals in a realistic way.

→ The programme includes a few strategies to address the challenges in programme participation.

→ The student's reflection is limited.

CBA Reflection Form – Strand 1

Consider using some of these words in your reflection:

Word Bank				
frequency	intensity	time	type	aerobic
anaerobic	muscular strength	muscular endurance	flexibility	speed
agility	specific	progressive	overload	reversible
rest and recovery	tedium	training zone	monitored	recorded
resilience	awareness	connected	responsible	managing myself

What kinds of physical activities do you enjoy and take part in regularly? (Review the *PE Passport*.)

Describe your health-related or performance-related fitness. (Review Fitness Test results.)

How would you rate your fitness? (Review the norms for age/gender.)

What are your training programme goals? Explain how they are SMART.
(Place S (Specific), M (Measurable), A (Achievable), R (Realistic), T (Time-bound), beside the point in the goal statement where each is demonstrated.)

Goal 1:

Goal 2:

Explain how your training programme is appropriate. (Review SPORRT principles.)

Specific:

Progressive:

Overload:

Reversibility:

Rest and Recovery:

Tedium:

What strategies did you use that demonstrate your ability to overcome setbacks?

Setback 1:

Strategy:

Setback 2:

Strategy:

Setback 3:

Strategy:

What are you most happy with about your experience?

Have you included a full profile of your health-related or performance-related physical activity (PA)?

My Fitness Programme

● I have identified the physical activity focus.	
● I have provided an overall PA profile – results/scores (see *PE Passport*).	
● I have made a comparison with norms for my age and gender.	
● I have stated my personal goals (more than one).	
● My goals are SMART.	
● My programme meets SPORRT principles.	
● I have completed my six-week programme.	

Reflection Review Checklist

● My reflection answers all questions.	
● I have named the strategies I used to help me stay on the programme.	
● I have explained my decisions/thinking/results. (I have avoided Yes/No answers.)	
● I have used appropriate terms to demonstrate my knowledge of health-related fitness.	

Signature:

Date:

STRAND 2

Games

Introduction to Games

Looking at it ☐   Working on it ☐   Nailed it ☐

Whether we participate in games for the competition, the craic or the company, the benefits that games bring to our lives are significant. In this strand you will play a wide range of games. You will challenge yourself to develop skills and understandings that will help you to participate in a confident, competent and safe way. You will adapt and lead games and activities for your classmates. Playing in teams is a large part of the game experience and you will examine how you can improve your team's performance. You will play types of games where you have to make tactical decisions and respond to your opponents' play.

Participating in games will have a significant health benefit and will help you to meet your MVPA target (60 minutes of moderate to vigorous physical activity) in a fun way. There is a game to suit everybody. Here's an opportunity to find yours.

> 'Life is more fun if you play games.'
> *Roald Dahl*

I wonder Why is one activity called a sport and another a game, e.g. wrestling and rugby?

My thoughts: _____

_____

At the end of this strand I will be able to:

Learning Outcomes Strand 2		Year 1	Year 2	Year 3
2.1	Use a wide range of movement skills and strategies effectively to enhance my performance			
2.2	Take responsibility for improving my own performance based on personal strengths and developmental needs			
2.3	Modify activities to promote inclusion and enjoyment in a safe manner			
2.4	Demonstrate activities to enhance my health-related and/or performance-related fitness for the particular game, including warm-up and cool-down			
2.5	Respond, individually and as part of a team, to different games' scenarios			

Class Challenge:

My Personal Challenge:

Games terminology

Fair play	Respecting the rules of the game and the right of all players to a fair competition.
Offence	The period of play and principles applied when a team/player is attacking the opponent's area with the aim of scoring. Also known as attack.
Defence	The period of play and principles applied when a team/player is preventing the opposition from scoring.
Strategy	An overall approach and plan where various tactics are combined and adopted to achieve a specific goal.
Tactic	An individual response to a particular situation as it arises in the game in order to outwit or overcome an opponent.
Evasion	The ability to lose touch with or avoid an opponent.
Anticipate	To predict where the next movement might be and move to receive or intercept.
Technique	A set of particular movements related to the demonstration of a skill.
Inclusion	Doing things that promote sports equally together and not merely alongside each other.
Fielding	Catching or picking up a ball/frisbee in the field after it has been hit or thrown in a game.

What qualities do you think these nominees for Young Player of the Year demonstrate? Check out the word bank on page 105 to give you some ideas.

1		5	
2		6	
3		7	
4		8	

vision	anticipation	endurance
short and stocky	can lift heavy weights	agility
explosive speed	tactically aware	excellent balance
highly skilful	size	self-belief
gritty and resilient	disciplined	team player

Fair Play Charter

When taking part in games it is important that all participants are free from fear of ridicule or threat. Think about how you can be a good sport, respect your opponent and respect officials. Draw up an **I will** and **I won't** fair play charter that will make everyone's experience of games a better one.

In order to promote fair play and a positive sporting environment in our school games, I promise that …

I will:

_____

_____

_____

I won't:

_____

_____

_____

What is the role of the referee in the game?

_____

_____

Keeping Your Head

Imagine that you are Robert and you have just experienced the incident described below. When you have read it, respond as honestly as possibly to the questions that follow.

Robert has just finished playing the second pool match in the class tournament. His team have lost again and his frustration has got the better of him.

'You're a bunch of losers! How many times do I pass the ball forward? And all you do is mess it up! You're the worst, Jack. You let the team down every week. And you're no better, Daniel. I don't know why I bother. We're going to get beaten again and it serves us right. This is rubbish and the referee can't do his job either. I'm not shaking his hand or anyone's hand for that matter.'

1 What did you think when you realised you had just lost your temper?	
2 What impact did the outburst have on you and others?	
3 What has been the hardest thing for you?	
4 What do you think needs to happen to make things right?	

5 What strategies could you use to help you remain in control?

My control strategies

Categories of Games

In the Junior Cycle specification, games are categorised into three different types:

→ Invasion games

→ Striking and fielding games

→ Divided court games.

Using your knowledge of how games are similar and different, put each of the following games into its correct category type.

→ basketball

→ badminton

→ rounders

→ cricket

→ table tennis

→ camogie

→ hockey

→ tennis

→ lacrosse

→ rugby

→ soccer

→ ultimate frisbee

→ softball

→ volleyball

→ Gaelic football

→ Olympic handball

→ hurling

→ baseball

→ futsal

→ water polo

→ pickleball

→ softball

Categories of Games		
Invasion games	**Striking and fielding games**	**Divided court games**

There is also another category of games — wall/shared court games.

Wall games/shared court games

Game	Distinguishing features
Handball Squash	• Using the wall to place the ball where the opponent will find difficulty returning it • A score is made when a player fails to return the ball within the number of bounces allowed • The ball must be struck and not carried • There is a section of the wall that must be played. A point is lost when the ball is played outside this area • Games are played solo or in pairs • A special type of ball is used • The winner is the one who gets to the points scored target first

Getting to Know Your Sport

> **LO 2.4** Demonstrate activities to enhance your health-related and/or performance-related fitness for the particular game, including warm-up and cool-down.

You can take charge of your own fitness development and devise exercises that will help you improve your health-related and/or performance-related fitness. You become the coach and take responsibility for the activities and/or skills that you need to practise.

First you need to understand the mix of fitness components that make up your sport.

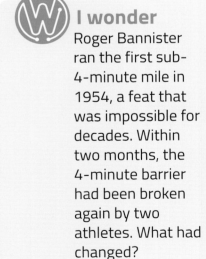

I wonder

Roger Bannister ran the first sub-4-minute mile in 1954, a feat that was impossible for decades. Within two months, the 4-minute barrier had been broken again by two athletes. What had changed?

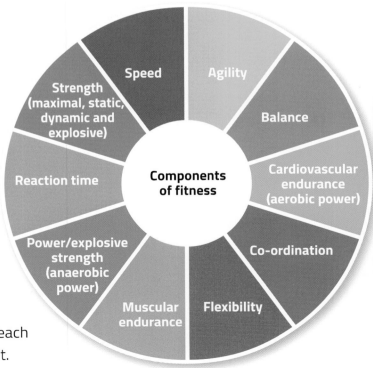

You can prioritise your training by deciding on the importance of each component of fitness in your sport.

Identify the level of each component using the following grading system:

1 = Low   2 = Low to moderate   3 = Moderate

4 = Moderate to high   5 = High

The components you rate as high or moderate to high will be the ones you target most. An analysis of your team performance will also help you to select the components in need of attention. There are blank spaces for your own games selections.

Health-related fitness (HRF)							
	Basketball	Gaelic football	Rounders	Volleyball	Badminton		
Cardiovascular endurance							
Strength							
Muscular endurance							
Flexibility							

Performance-related fitness (PRF)							
	Basketball	Gaelic football	Rounders	Volleyball	Badminton		
Agility							
Balance							
Co-ordination							
Reaction time							
Speed							
Power							

Organise and Run Drills to Develop an Aspect of HRF or PRF

You need a plan of action to run your activity well. With your teacher, form the teams for your class. Each team will select the fitness component they would like to focus on and then the drill or activity they plan to run. Here is an example. Try it out and then you can go about planning your own.

Example

Activity:	Ball handling			
Organising team:	Ruth L.	Tomás M.	Tadhg P.	Eibhlín Ní M.
Focus of fitness:	HRF ☐	PRF ✓		
Component:	Co-ordination			
Organisation:	Groups of three. Relay formation. Cones set 10–15 m apart.			
Equipment:	4 cones, 2 tennis balls, 2 larger balls, per group			

Drill or activity description:

- Begin with students in groups of three at the sideline.
- One player reverses while the other two jog forward, keeping a distance of 1–2 m apart.
- Players jogging forward pass a ball one at a time to the reversing player.
- The reversing player receives and returns the ball to the same player.
- On arriving at the end line, change the reversing player.
- Change the ball and/or the pace of the drill.

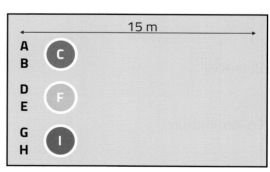

What helped me to explain the drill? _____

Why? _____

Something that surprised me: _____

Now try this.

Activity:	Freeze tag
Organising team:	
Focus of fitness:	HRF ☐ PRF ☐
Component:	Muscular endurance and agility
Organisation:	Groups of eight: six players wear tags; two are taggers – chase runners. Area 10 m x 10 m.
Equipment:	6 bibs, 4 cones, 6 tags, 6 rugby balls per group

Drill or activity description:

- Each runner carries a ball, holding it in both hands.

- When a player is tagged they must freeze and place their ball at their feet.

- Frozen players can be released by taking and returning a pass from a free player.

- Add an additional tagger to make it harder.

- Change taggers regularly – their function is physically demanding.

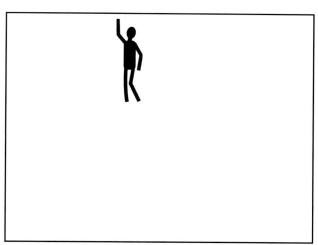

In the box, draw stickpeople to copy the image below.

How did you avoid being tagged?

How can taggers work together to tag a player?

111

Now devise your own activity.

Activity:

Organising team:

Focus of fitness: HRF ☐   PRF ☐

Component:

Organisation:

Equipment:

Drill or activity description:

-
-
-
-
-
-
-

My activity

Inclusive Activities

LO 2.3 Modify activities to promote inclusion and enjoyment in a safe manner.

Everybody has different strengths and weaknesses. Changing activities to make sure everybody is included and enjoying themselves is very important.

I wonder How is the task set by the examiner unfair to the participants?

How can you help? What parts of any activity could you change to include more people?

My thoughts:

1 _____

2 _____

3 _____

4 _____

5 _____

You can use the acronym CHANGE IT to help you make your games more inclusive.

Let's CHANGE IT!

C	Coaching style	Is the activity suited to the abilities of all my classmates or only some of them? Is it complicated or easy for everyone to understand?
H	How to score or win!	Are there different ways to score? Can you get more points from different positions?
A	Area you play in	Does the space to play need to be bigger or smaller? Are there set distances between players and targets?
N	Number of players	How many players on each team? Is it harder with more or fewer players?
G	Game rules	Are the rules easy or hard to apply? Are you changing the rules to make the game more/less challenging?
E	Equipment	Would the size, shape and feel of equipment make a difference? Is the net too high or too low? Is different equipment available for different abilities?
I	Inclusion	How many people have to touch the ball before scoring? Could players have specific positions or roles? Could they have specific space to work in?
T	Time	Is the duration of the game too short/long? Do you have to score within a certain amount of time (e.g. 30 seconds)?

Visit www.sportaus.gov.au/p4l to access Playing for Life activity cards, which contain fun and enlightening games revolving around sport.

Four corners

Play the Four Corners game. Based on your experience, use CHANGE IT to change any three elements and make the game more inclusive.

Game Name:	Number of Players:

Brief explanation:
The aim is to score in the corners of the playing area.

What equipment you need:
- Cones
- Balls
- Bibs

Diagram:

How you play:

- Put a cone in each corner of a square/rectangle the size of a badminton court.
- You cannot move with the ball.
- You regain possession by intercepting the ball.
- Non-contact, no tackling.
- Players cannot wait at/remain in a corner.

Safety:

- Keep cones away from the wall so that players have space to slow down.
- Make sure the area is clear of loose equipment.
- No jewellery or untied shoelaces.

CHANGE IT:

C _____

H _____

A _____

N _____

G _____

E _____

I _____

T _____

Scoring:

- You score by catching the ball in the corner. You must step into the corner as you catch the ball.
- Players try to score in all four corners.

Ask the players:

- Discuss the level of physicality in the game.

Now give your modified game a go!

Reflection

What did you do to make sure people were safe?

_____

_____

What would you change to make the game more interesting?

_____

_____

What would you change to make it easier or harder?

_____

_____

Was your game inclusive? How do you know?

_____

_____

115

Games Making

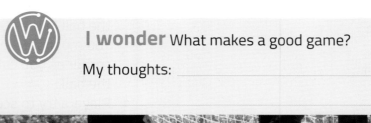

I wonder What makes a good game?

My thoughts: _____

_____

'A game is an experience created by rules'
Anna Anthropy

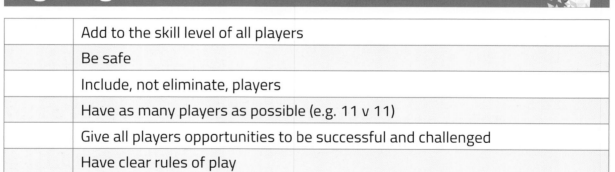

In this task you are going to create your own game. Make sure you consider these points.

Which do you think are the most important? Number them from 1 (most important) to 6 (least important).

A good game should ...

	Add to the skill level of all players
	Be safe
	Include, not eliminate, players
	Have as many players as possible (e.g. 11 v 11)
	Give all players opportunities to be successful and challenged
	Have clear rules of play

What's your number one and why?

_____

_____

Create your game

In this activity you will introduce and lead a game you have created. Here are some things to remember!

Before the game:

→ Introduce the game

→ Explain how to play

→ What are the safety rules?

→ Give a demonstration

→ Any questions?

During the game:

→ Watch and take note if you need to CHANGE IT

→ Stop the game and explain if anything is misunderstood

After the game:

→ Ask players what they thought and what they learned from the game

→ Consider if it was a good game

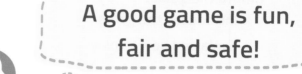

A good game is fun, fair and safe!

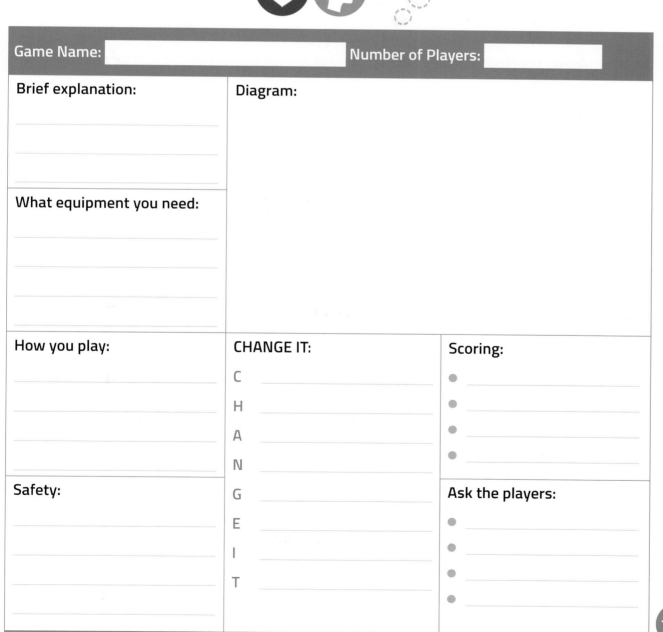

Game Name: _____   Number of Players: _____

Brief explanation:
_____
_____
_____

What equipment you need:
_____
_____
_____

Diagram:

How you play:
_____
_____
_____

Safety:
_____
_____
_____

CHANGE IT:

C _____

H _____

A _____

N _____

G _____

E _____

I _____

T _____

Scoring:

• _____

• _____

• _____

• _____

Ask the players:

• _____

• _____

• _____

• _____

Feedback

Now you're going to help your classmate make small changes to improve by giving them feedback on their performance. Answer the questions below based on your experience of their game.

Name of the game: _____

Tick the boxes if they did the following:

Before the game:

→ Introduced the game ☐   → Gave a demonstration ☐

→ Explained how to play ☐   → Asked if there were any questions ☐

→ Laid out the safety rules ☐

During the game:

→ Watched the game closely and stopped it when necessary ☐

→ Asked the players if they needed more of a challenge or needed it to be easier ☐

After the game:

→ Asked the players what they thought and what they might change ☐

Mark these elements of the game on a scale of 1–5 based on which statement it is closest to.

Boring	1 2 3 4 5	Exciting
Too many players	1 2 3 4 5	Not enough players
Too difficult	1 2 3 4 5	Too easy
Hard to understand the rules	1 2 3 4 5	Clear rules
Unfair refereeing	1 2 3 4 5	Completely fair refereeing
Unsafe	1 2 3 4 5	Safe
Scoring was impossible	1 2 3 4 5	Scoring was too easy
Playing area was too big/small	1 2 3 4 5	Playing area was just right
Inactive	1 2 3 4 5	Highly active

Now let's pick out two stars and a wish.

→ **Two stars:** Two things that went well.

→ **A wish:** One thing they could do differently to improve their game and delivery next time.

Warm-up

A thorough warm-up will take at least 10 minutes – maybe longer, depending on weather conditions and context. The warm-up should provide a smooth transition from rest to game/competition pace. The warm-up should finish just before the main activity or event. There are three distinct phases to an effective warm-up.

Think **RFM**.

→ **Raise heart rate:** Gradual pulse-raising activities – jog, fast walk, increasing the amount of oxygen to the working muscles.

→ **Flexibility:** Stretching all relevant muscles and actively mobilising the joints. Begin with the upper body and finish with the lower body. Static stretches should be held for 7–10 seconds.

→ **Mobility and movement rehearsal:** Include the movement skills and techniques actually used in the activity/game, e.g. dribbling a ball to warm up for a basketball game.

Which of the following statements are true (✓) or false (✗)?

The warm-up …	True or false?
Concentrates the mind by rehearsing the movement patterns in the game	
Decreases the amount of lactic acid in the muscles and reduces the likelihood of muscle soreness	
Stretches the muscles, moves the joints and increases the range of movement, reducing the likelihood of injury or strain	
Increases the blood flow to the muscles, raising the temperature of the body, in preparation for the activity to follow	

In groups of three, lead an effective warm-up. Each person takes responsibility for one phase of the warm-up. The warm-up must be specific to the game in hand. Fill in the planning form below. Use diagrams and images to help remind you of the activities.

Our warm-up		
Phase	Description	Diagram/image
Raise heart rate		
Flexibility		
Mobility and movement rehearsal		

How do you know that your warm-up was successful?

What was the best part about leading this activity? Why?

What was the hardest part? Why?

Stretching guidelines

It is important that the stretching is gradual, with no violent movement, so that no muscles are damaged. This will enable you to conduct the warm-up and cool-down safely. Stretching incorrectly by forcing the stretch or stretching out of balance is not good for you. During warm-up, static stretches should be held for 7–10 seconds.

Think **SEAM**!

→ **S**tability: The body should be in balance and steady.

→ **E**ffectiveness: Isolate the muscles, ligaments and joints and use the correct technique.

→ **A**lignment: Avoid twisting; keep limbs in line.

→ **M**omentum: Use controlled movement; avoid bouncing.

Static stretching

Cool-down

Cooling down performs a number of really important functions in your body's recovery and adaptation to training.

With a partner, see how many benefits of a cool-down you can think of.

The cool-down period helps:

_____

_____

_____

An effective cool-down should include:

→ A gradual reduction in intensity, e.g. run → light jog → walk.

→ Stretching of all main muscle groups used in the activity.

Fill in the table below with a description and diagrams or images of the cool-down process.

Cool-down		
Phase	**Description**	**Diagram/image**
Heart rate		
Stretching		

Recovery time

After a period of exercise, it may take some time to recover and return to your normal steady state. Recovery time will depend on how intense and strenuous the exercise was and your initial level of fitness. A number of things happen in this recovery period.

Heart rate: Falls back to its normal rate when you stop exercising. The fitter you are the faster it falls.

Muscle repair: May be needed, depending on collisions and impact, and will need time.

Lactic acid: Needs to be removed. Lots of oxygen is needed to get rid of it.

Glycogen stores: May be run down and could take up to 48 hours to be restored.

> **LO 2.1** Use a wide range of movement skills and strategies effectively to enhance my performance.

All invasion games have a number of similar contexts that can be prepared for tactically. The tactical problems revolve around three key elements:

1. Winning possession
2. Keeping and progressing possession
3. Scoring.

Think about a team that is very successful and consider how they have mastered these elements. List the tactics they demonstrate in the columns below.

Tactical solutions: Invasion games		
My chosen team:		
Winning possession	**Keeping and progressing possession**	**Scoring**

I wonder 'Attack wins games but defence wins championships.' What do you think?

My thoughts: _____

On the next page, we'll look at each of the tactical problems that arise in invasion games.

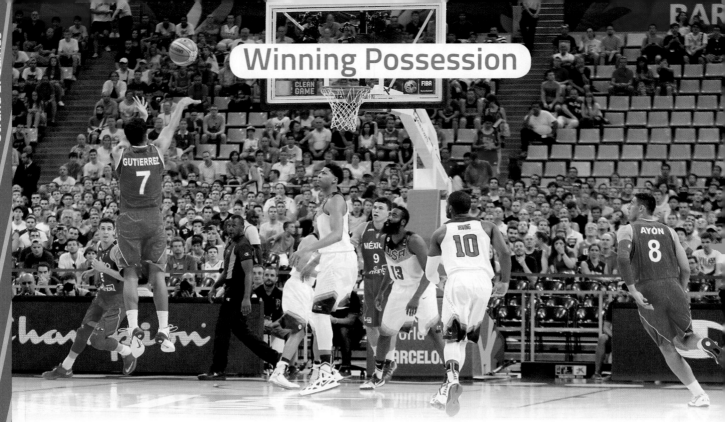

Winning Possession

Read the game

Focus: Closing down space; anticipating passing lines.

The game: A 2 v 2 possession game in a 10 m x 10 m playing area. The aim of the game is to make five consecutive passes. Focus on what tactics you can adopt in order to regain possession.

Rules:

→ Non-contact.

→ Your choice of ball – basketball, football, netball, etc.

→ You can move with the ball – dribble.

→ Restart is from the sideline where ball leaves the boundary.

→ If there is an intercept or the ball goes out of bounds, the other team gains possession.

	First defender	Second defender
How did you win the ball back?		
How did you close down space?		

Team tag

Focus: Defensive teamwork and strategic positioning to close down space.

The game: Play a 4 v 4 tag game. Try to tag the opposition team within a 2-minute time limit. One ball per team.

Playing area: 15 m x 15 m.

Rules:

→ You cannot move with the ball in hand.

→ You are tagged when you are touched by a player when you are in possession of the ball.

→ You are not permitted to hold or impede an opposing player.

→ Moving outside the boundary results in being tagged.

→ When tagged, stand still with your hands out. To release you, one of your teammates must run around you.

→ Count the number of players 'stuck' when the time is up.

	Player with the ball	Players without the ball
How did you close down space?		
How did you communicate the next move?		
How did you get into a good tagging position?		
Why did your team play break down?		

Time zones

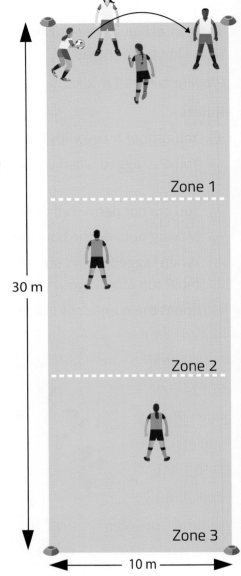

Focus: Selecting appropriate defensive strategies; exploring the role of individual players.

The game: Teams of three. The playing area is 30 m x 10 m divided into three zones of 10 m x 10 m. Begin with the attacking team at one end and one defender in each zone. In the second zone the defence will be increased to two, with the first defender joining the waiting defender to make a 3 v 2 game. In the third zone the defence will be increased to make a 3 v 3 game. There is a playing time limit of 1 minute per zone.

Scoring:

Five consecutive passes:

    in Zone 1 = 1 point

    in Zone 2 = 2 points

    in Zone 3 = 3 points

Two lots of five consecutive passes in Zone 2 = 4 points.

The team with the most points wins.

Rules:

→ If the ball is dropped, out of bounds or intercepted, begin from zero in that zone.

→ No movement allowed with ball in hand.

→ Teams move to the next zone after 1 minute in the previous zone.

→ Non-contact.

Time Zone Tally			
Team name:			
Zone 1	**Zone 2**	**Zone 3**	**Tally**

In defending each zone, the demands are different. You need to consider how to work best as a defence and adopt effective defence strategies suited to each context.

	Defence preview	Defence review
How will you/did you prevent the other team scoring?		
What tactics will you/did you use in each zone to minimise the offence score?		
How will you/did you force the offence to delay the pass?		
How will you/did you work together?		

How would you rate your team's performance of the following skills in defence? Rate from 1 (nailed it) to 5 (skills are poor and have a significant impact on defence).

Invasion games: Defence skills analysis		
Skill	Rating	Our target for improvement
Footwork		
Marking and closing down		
Tackling and challenging		
Anticipating and intercepting		

Now think how you could improve your defence skills.

Skill	My personal target for improvement
Footwork	
Marking and intercepting	
Tackling and challenging	
Anticipating and intercepting	

Snapshot

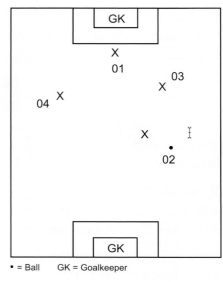

This is a 5 v 5 game which has been frozen in time. **You are team X** defending against team O. Examine the defence positions in response to the position of each member of the offence, O1–O4. O2 has the ball. Answer the questions that follow.

• = Ball   GK = Goalkeeper

How will you:

Stop the attack?

_____

_____

Increase your chances of regaining possession?

_____

_____

Reduce the opposition's scoring opportunity?

_____

_____

Consider using some of these words:

anticipate	intercept	close down space	reconsider
slow down	reorganise	communicate	pressure the ball
person-to-person defence	goal-side	cover the angle	focus

Skill development

> **LO 2.2** Take responsibility for improving my own performance based on personal strengths and developmental needs.

Where you have recognised a skill limitation, either individual or team, you have a responsibility to work to deal with it. You will need to look at the skill in more detail and identify what makes a successful move or execution of that skill.

Here is an example to help you. Be aware of your defensive footwork and stance. Play the game and see if you recognise what makes effective defence movements. Your teacher will work with you to confirm the criteria.

Working to improve: defensive stance and movement

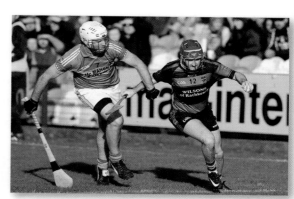

Work with a partner in a 10 m x 10 m grid. The attacking player wears a tag and attempts to move past the defender and through the mini-goal, maintaining the tag. Begin 5 m apart. Stand directly opposite your partner. Aim to shadow your partner by reacting to their movement as quickly as possible. Make three attempts before switching.

Identify what helps your defensive movements, i.e. your criteria for effective defensive movement and stance. Write down the criteria you agree with your teacher on the Observation Form below.

Now do the activity again, using the peer observation form to receive some feedback on your performance. Tick the **P/E (present/effective)** box every time your partner demonstrates the criterion. Tick **A/I (absent/inappropriate)** whenever a criterion is not demonstrated.

Invasion Games Observation Form

Observer name:		Review date:	
Activity/skill:			
Criteria:		**Record of performance**	
		P/E	A/I
1			
2			
3			
4			

Taking these observations on board, identify:

One thing you are doing well:

A SMART performance goal:

I wonder What is the fastest ball sport in the world?

My thoughts: _____

_____

Games analysis: defence

Use the form below to analyse the effectiveness of your team's defence. Have a team stats analyst observe your game play, indicating the standard of each element of defence. Put a tick in the appropriate coloured section as you see it happen in the course of the game.

Green = In good shape   Orange = Some issues   Red = In need of attention

Winning possession	Anticipation	Tackling	Pressuring ball carrier
Comments:			
Organising defence	Marking	Zone defence	Person-to-person
Comments:			
Defending the goal/ area	Goalkeeper	Cover	Clearance/outlet
Comments:			
Set plays (game-specific)	1_____	2_____	3_____
Comments:			

Taking these observations on board, identify:

One thing you are doing well:

_____

A SMART performance goal:

_____

Keeping and Progressing Possession

Once possession has been secured, it is important to attack the opponent's territory and set up the opportunity for a score. Possession needs to be carefully maintained through good decision-making and efficient execution of skills. Important questions here include: How do we keep possession? How do we invade the opponent's territory? The following games are designed to focus on keeping and progressing possession.

Piggy in the middle

Focus: When to pass, and when to pass and when to hold; supporting the player in possession.

The game: Play a 3 v 1 game in one half of a badminton court. One player begins as 'piggy in the middle'. Aim to make as many passes as possible within a 30-second time limit.

Rules:

→ Non-contact.

→ Own choice of ball – basketball, hockey ball, etc.

→ Players are not permitted to move with the ball.

→ Any interception or out of bounds throw returns score to zero.

→ Change defence player after each bout.

Player in possession	
How did you keep possession?	
Player without the ball	
How did you signal for a pass?	
How did you support the player in possession?	
Why did your team play break down?	

Funnel-ball

Focus: Exploring the advantage of width and speed in attack.

The game: Play 3 v 3. Players play touch rugby on a funnel-shaped pitch. One team begins by attacking the wide goal line. A score is made by crossing the goal line untagged. Each team's direction of attack is changed regularly.

Rules:

→ Players can pass in any direction.

→ When tagged with two hands, the ball must be passed immediately.

→ Each team has five attempts to cross the opponent's goal line.

→ Kicking the ball ahead is not permitted.

→ Devise your own system of re-start.

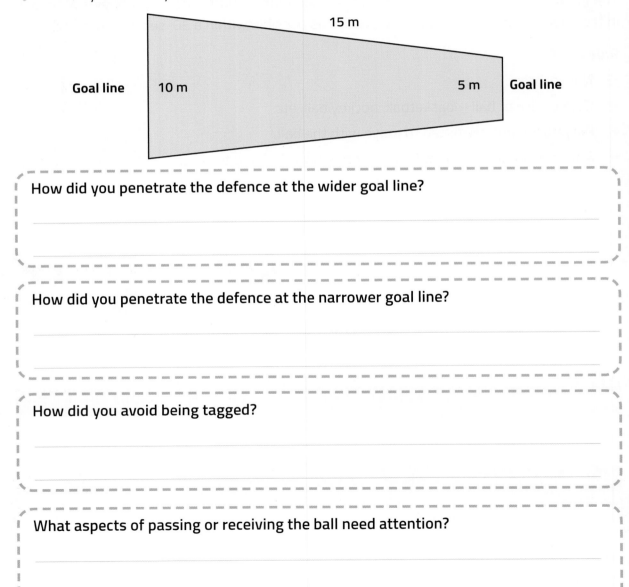

How did you penetrate the defence at the wider goal line?

How did you penetrate the defence at the narrower goal line?

How did you avoid being tagged?

What aspects of passing or receiving the ball need attention?

Wing man

Focus: Width, support, penetration.

The game: Three sets of two players: two defenders; two infield attackers; and two wing attackers. These roles will change throughout the game. The playing area is 14 m x 14 m, inclusive of the wings (2 m wide on either side). The attacking team aims to score by throwing the ball into the goal. Following a successful attack, the defending team changes to the wings, the attacking infield team become defenders and the wing players become the infield attack. The game continues immediately.

Rules:

→ Players cannot move with ball in hand.

→ Wing players cannot score.

→ Non-contact.

→ If the defence intercepts, they attack immediately and can use the wing players.

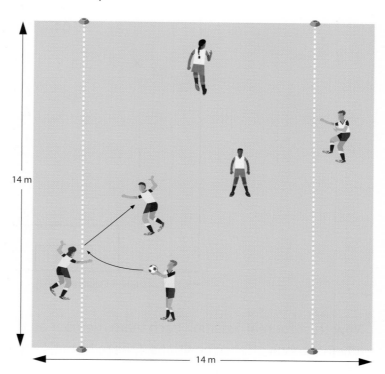

How did you move the ball forward quickly?

How did you use the wings to your advantage?

Why would you move the ball wide?

Snapshot

This is a 5 v 5 game that has been frozen in time. **You are team O** attacking against defending team X. Examine the current offence positions in relation to the position of the ball. O2 has the ball. Draw arrows to indicate where each player should move in order to receive the ball safely and become an attacking threat.

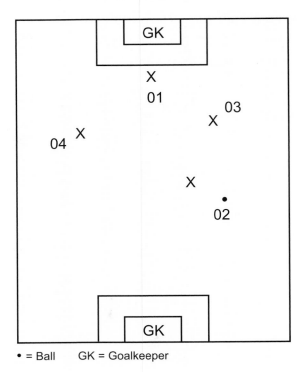

• = Ball   GK = Goalkeeper

Now try it for real. Position each team member as they are in the diagram. Move into more advantageous offence positions. Freeze frame. Now re-set the defence and freeze frame again.

How did you:

Improve the attack?

_____

_____

Increase your chances of scoring?

_____

_____

Reduce the chance of turning over possession?

_____

_____

Scoring

Once you have gained advantage in the opponent's territory, you will work to create the opportunity to shoot and score. Attacking the target by penetrating the defence will provide the opening for the shot at goal. In this moment you will need to create the space to shoot accurately. It will also be important to take advantage of set pieces.

What qualities do these high-scoring players demonstrate?

```
My thoughts:
_____

_____
```

Diamond

Focus: Taking shooting opportunities.

The game: The pitch is marked out in a diamond shape, 30 m x 40 m. The modified pitch provides more scoring opportunities. Attacking players must use the width of the pitch to create clear shooting opportunities and to shoot whenever the chance presents itself. A variety of shots are possible: driven shots from in front of the goal; curled shots from distance; angled drives across the goal, etc.

Rules:

→ Two teams of four.

→ Play full game conditions.

→ Officiate as per game regulations.

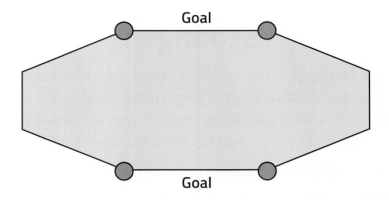

Goal

Goal

Where do you want to get the ball for the best shot at goal? Why?

How can your team get the ball there?

What leads to shooting breakdown?

Observer brief:

1. Analyse shooting issues.

2. Which of the following elements causes most concern?

Feedback Form – Shooting

Observer name:		Review date:
Issue	**Comment**	
Lack of skill		
Taking too long		
One-footedness/one-sided		
Selecting wrong shot		
Lack of strength in the shot		

Rover

Focus: When and where to shoot?

The game: Five players per team play a passing game aiming to score in the opposite team's goal. Each team nominates two attackers, two defenders and one 'rover'. Only the rover can move across the mid-line. An attacker can call 'Shot on' at any point if they feel a good opportunity to score presents itself. All players must freeze until the shot is taken.

Equipment: Ball, e.g. basketball/handball; goals, basket or target.

Playing area: 10 m x 15 m playing area. Court divided at the mid-line. Court divided into two sections at the mid-line.

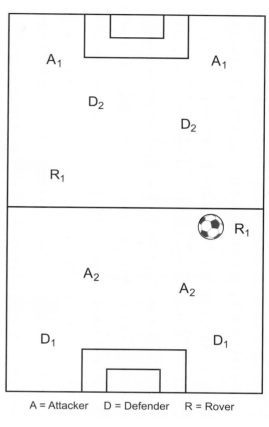

A = Attacker   D = Defender   R = Rover

Rules:

→ A player cannot move with the ball, i.e. dribble or run.

→ Non-contact.

→ Stripping the ball from a player is not allowed.

→ When 'Shot on' is called, the attacker may reposition their feet but they are not allowed to turn if facing away from the goal/target.

→ After a shot is taken, possession goes to the defenders.

→ Change the team roles after a time.

How do you lose the defender to make space for a shot?

Where is the best place to shoot from?

How do you support your teammates?

Games analysis: attack

Use this form to analyse the effectiveness of your team's defence. Have a team stats analyst observe your game play, indicating the standard of each element of attack. Put a tick in the appropriate coloured section as you see it happen in the course of the game.

Green = In good shape   Orange = Some issues   Red = In need of attention

Maintaining possession	Passing (choice and execution)	Communication	Support for ball carrier
Comments:			

Progressing the attack	Go forward with ball	Width/depth	Overlapping runs
Comments:			

Attacking the goal/area	Shot choice	Penetration	Rebounds/follow up
Comments:			

Set plays (game-specific)	1 _____	2 _____	3 _____
Comments:			

Striking and Fielding Games

> **LO 2.1** Use a wide range of movement skills and strategies effectively to enhance my performance.

In this category of games, each team plays offence or defence at any one time. Defence players aim to keep the striking team's score to a minimum. Offensive players aim to place the ball to their best advantage in order to score.

What do you know about the demands of this category of games? What do you need in order to be successful in these games?

Game awareness		
Tactical decision-making	**Skills**	**Rules**

> *i*   Many familiar sayings come from the language of baseball. 'Throw a curve ball' means coming up with something unexpected that requires a quick reaction. Something that comes 'out of left field' is something unusual and unexpected.

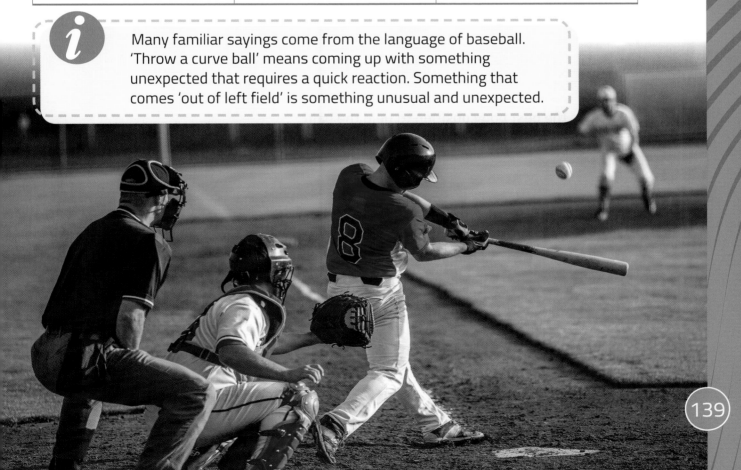

Bowled over

Focus: Ball placement and fielding decisions.

The game: Groups of five play a 4 v 1 game on a pitch 10 m wide and 20 m+ long.

Cones mark the boundary and the target lines for one run (10 m), four runs (15 m) and six runs (20 m+). Each player has the opportunity to bat and receives six pitched balls (an over) from each member of the group (24 balls in total). The backstop (the person behind the batter) is changed after each over. The batter's score is calculated by the area the ball is struck into, minus fielders' points.

Equipment: Cones; base mats for bowling and batting; cricket bat and stumps; ball (tennis ball/softball).

Rules:

→ The ball must be bowled underarm.

→ The batter loses five runs if they are bowled out or the ball is caught in flight.

→ The ball must strike the ground within the boundary.

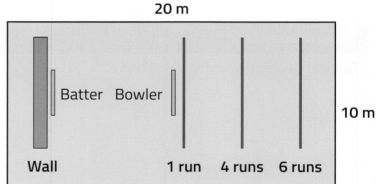

What is the best body position for batting?

What is the best body position to field the ball?

How do you decide which zone to attack?

Do you alter your fielding position for different batters? Why/why not?

Mini-rounders

Focus: Developing decision-making.

The game: Two teams, three on each team, one team fielding and one striking. Playing area is fan-shaped. Fourth base is the home base. Each striker aims to strike the ball to land within the boundary and then to run from base to base to get home. Fielders attempt to get the player out or restrict the number of bases the player will run to. Each base is worth 1 point. A home run scores 4 points.

Equipment: Cones or hoops for bases; base mats for pitching and batting; rounders bat; ball (tennis ball/softball).

Rules:

→ If a player misses with two swings they must walk to first base – no points.

→ Player must make contact with the base to be safe.

→ A player cannot pass out a teammate.

→ Runners must not be impeded.

→ A 'fair ball' is pitched between knee and shoulder height. If three bad balls are pitched in a row, all batting players walk forward to the next base.

→ A player is got out by catching the ball cleanly in flight; contacting the base to which the player is running, with ball in hand; or touching the player with ball in hand.

→ Drop the bat at the base before running.

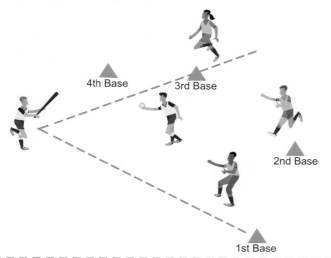

4th Base 3rd Base 2nd Base 1st Base

Which base should you tag first? Why?

141

What is the best way to get the ball to the base?

_____

_____

How do you best defend the space?

_____

_____

How do you make time and space for your run as a batter?

_____

_____

How far should you run? Why?

_____

_____

This rounders match has been frozen in time. Your team are batting. There are no 'outs' on the team. You have a runner at 1st base. You are only allowed to hit the ball infield to 'the green zone'. Examine the options for batters and fielders. Answer the questions that follow.

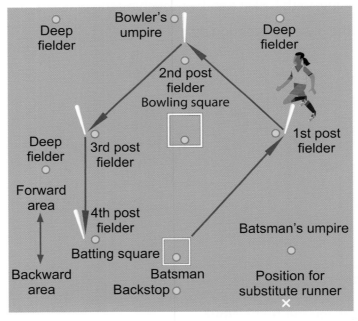

Where should the batter hit the ball? Why?

_____

_____

Where should the fielders position themselves?

Where should the fielders aim to get the batter out?

Striking and fielding games feedback form

Using the rating scale below, select a number of stars from 1 to 5 to indicate your opinion of the batting and fielding of another team: 5 = very strong; 3 = moderate; 1 = weak.

Observer name:	Review date: ☐☐ ☐☐ ☐☐
Success factor	**Your rating**
Fielding	
Fielded cleanly and threw to base	☆☆☆☆☆
Provided cover to the fielder at base	☆☆☆☆☆
Communicated – showed target hands	☆☆☆☆☆
2nd base tagged outside base and stood in line with thrower	☆☆☆☆☆
Looked up, scanned and decided a play	☆☆☆☆☆
Batting	
Got to 1st base and got 1st base player to 2nd	☆☆☆☆☆
Hit the right ball for the situation	☆☆☆☆☆
Base runners decided whether to stay or run	☆☆☆☆☆

What are the team doing well ...

As batters?

As fielders?

What do the team need to improve on for the next game ...

As batters?

As fielders?

LO 2.1 Use a wide range of movement skills and strategies effectively to enhance their performance.

Sitting Volleyball

Go to YouTube and search for 'Sitting Volleyball Video' (0:33).

Play the game and complete the game analysis sheet. Take note of what is distinctive about the game. It represents some of the main elements of this category of game.

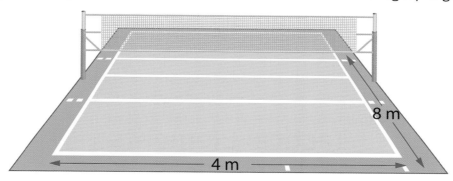

8 m

4 m

Equipment: Volleyball, net.

Organisation: Two teams of six.

Playing area: 8 m x 4 m. Net at height of 1.5 m separates the teams.

Rules:

→ Game begins with a serve (two-handed throw) from behind the back line.

→ All players seated on the floor.

→ Players cannot move with ball in hand.

→ No limit to the number of touches before transferring the ball across the net.

→ Service is handed to the other team after a foul or three consecutive points.

→ Players rotate positions one place clockwise on regaining serve.

→ A score is made by getting the ball to hit the ground within the boundary on the opponents' side of the net.

Game analysis sheet: divided court games

Describe the playing area. (Shape, dimensions, indoor/outdoor, etc.)	
How do you score and win a game?	
How do you carry or move the ball?	
What do you have to think about if you have possession?	
Where is the best place to score from?	
What is the hardest shot to defend against? Why?	

I wonder Why is the net higher in volleyball than in badminton?

My thoughts: _____

_____

Tactical Elements
The 4Rs

Now we'll look at the 4Rs of divided court games and see how they connect to tactical problem-solving and decision-making.

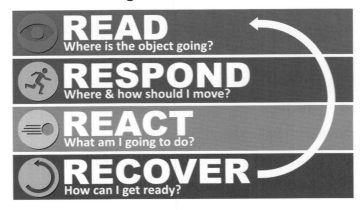

Now we are going to use the 4Rs to look at these tactical elements:

Consistency	Preparing to attack	Defending space	Scoring	Defending an attack

Consistency

Think about:

→ Positioning   → Footwork   → Accuracy

Hoop ball 1

Focus: *Read* and *Respond* to the placement of the ball by positioning yourself facing the target.

The game:

→ You have one ball and a target on the ground.

→ You bounce the ball off the ground, so it goes above head height, aiming at the target on the ground.

→ You must move to the opposite side of the target and catch the ball before it hits the ground.

Try to ... catch the ball facing the target.

Target

What was the best position to catch the ball? Why?	
What helped you to catch the ball successfully?	

Watch this video and answer the question below.

Go to YouTube and search for 'ITTF Top 10 Table Tennis Points of 2013' (6:58).

What is the benefit of hitting the ball so high?

_____

_____

Hoop ball 2

Focus: *React* and *Respond* to where your opponent puts the ball and look for the space where they cannot reach it.

The game:

→ One against one or two against two.

→ You must catch the ball and bounce it in the centre zone.

→ The ball must bounce above head level.

→ You must throw from where you caught it.

→ If the ball hits the ground outside the centre zone, the thrower gets a point.

Try to ... stand opposite your opponent after you've thrown the ball.

	Player 1	Player 2
How did you move your opponent in order to score?		
How did recovering to stand opposite your opponent help?		
How can you anticipate where your opponent will throw the ball?		
Is it easier to move forwards or backwards when catching the ball? Why?		

Preparing to attack

Think about:

→ Playing the ball to create space

→ Corners/sides/front and back

→ Communication.

Watch these videos and answer the questions below.

Go to YouTube and search for 'ALL TEAM ATTACK Beautiful Volleyball Actions (HD)' (4:24)

How do these players prepare to attack and where do they attack from?

_____

_____

_____

What comes before their attack shot? How did this help them execute their final shot?

_____

_____

_____

Getting in the zone

Focus: Pressuring your opponent to *React* and *Recover* quickly by targeting different areas of the court.

The game:

→ You and your opponent will be in a zoned area with a net between you.

→ If your ball/shuttle lands in the back zone it is worth 4, the middle zone 1 and the front zone 3.

→ The first player to reach 21 points wins.

Try to ... move your opponent.

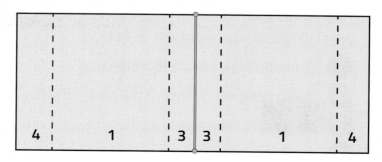

List the shots that will be useful in this game and describe their use.

Shot	Use

	Player 1	Player 2
Where did you force your opponent to move to in order to create space on court?		
How did you give your opponent less time to recover?		
How did you give yourself time to recover?		
Where is the best place on the court to recover to? Why?		

Reflection

How would you rate your performance of the following skills in offence? In the table on page 151, score each element as follows:

1 Limited, rarely seen and ineffective.

2 Acceptable, seen most of the time, effective.

3 Very good, seen nearly all the time, very effective.

4 Excellent, seen all the time, extremely effective.

Offensive skills analysis		
Skills and tactics	Score	My target for improvement
Positioning		
Communication		
Varied placement of shots		
Moving my opponent		
Footwork		
Range of game shots/skills		

Defending space

Think about:

→ Recovery position and anticipation

→ Formations

Watch this video and answer the questions that follow.

Go to YouTube and search for 'BADMINTON: THE DYNAMIC CENTER, POSITION SINGLES #31' (1:55).

Where did the player return to after all the shots?

_____

_____

What is the benefit of moving back to this position?

_____

_____

The shaded areas in the courts below (A–E) represent your defensive position. Connect them with scenarios 1–5 and write each letter in the appropriate box.

1	Receiving serve	
2	Opponents attacking from front court on right	
3	Opponents attacking from front court in centre	
4	Opponents attacking from front court on left	
5	Opponents attacking from back court	

Court aware

Focus: *Read* and *Respond* to specific areas in order to protect space in a game situation.

The game:

→ One against one or two against two.

→ You will play a short game.

→ Your partner will draw on maps of the court below where you are standing in each of the following scenarios.

Try to ... be aware of where your partner is standing.

1	Receiving serve		
2	Opponent(s) attacking from front court on right		
3	Opponent(s) attacking from front court in centre		
4	Opponent(s) attacking from front court on left		
5	Opponent(s) attacking from back court		

Based on your partner's mapping, answer the following questions:

How many times were you in the right place? _____

How did your positioning when defending impact on your game?

_____

_____

How did your positioning affect your opponent's options? Give one example.

_____

_____

How did you make time for yourself to recover your position?

_____

Formations

What games are being played in the diagrams and why is the formation adopted in each case?

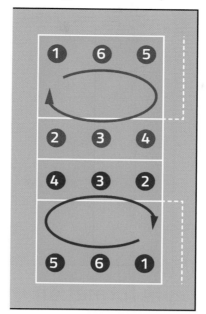

1

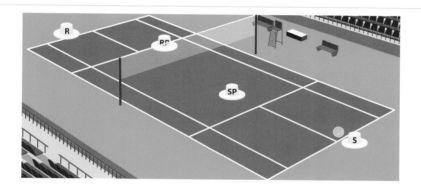

2

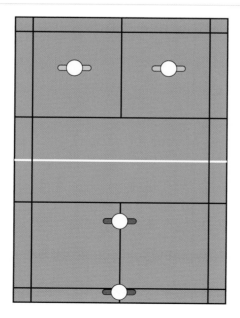

3

Below is your court. Depending on what divided court game you are playing, draw the formation your team would be in at the beginning of the game in attack/defence.

Formation in Attack	Formation in Defence

In formation

Give your formation a go!

Each person on your team will have the opportunity to try their formation. You will have two opportunities each to score.

Did your formation work well? Why/why not?

_____

_____

What were the advantages of your formation?

_____

_____

What were the disadvantages of your formation?

_____

_____

If you were to design it again, what would you do differently?

_____

_____

Scoring

Think about:

→ Choice of shot – speed, height, distance

→ Shot placement – at or between players, into clear space, near the net.

Watch this video and take note of what shot the player chooses, and where she places the shot.

Go to YouTube and search for 'Pv Sindhu best attacking shots' (5:10).

	Game 1	Game 2	Game 3
Choice of shot			
Speed			
Height			
Distance			
Shot placement			
At the player			
Clear space			
Near the net			

What made her shots so successful?

Now look at this fictional game.

Cormac just recently started playing. He is still learning the skills and is not 100% sure what's going on.

Tadgh is on the school team and this is his favourite sport.
He practises as often as possible and can't wait to get playing.

Your teammate enjoys playing. She likes to get involved,
her skills are good and she is creative when she plays.

You want to score and you are returning the net shot. You must
choose what shot and where to place it. Check the positions of
the players on the court diagram.

> **Explain what shot you will choose, where you will hit it and why you chose that tactic.**

Ground it

Focus: *Reading* the strengths and weaknesses of the players around you and choosing
shots and placements to win.

The game:

→ You are trying to get the ball/shuttle to land in your opponent's box.

→ If the ball/shuttle touches the ground in your box you lose a letter from the word
'SCORING'.

→ You are not allowed enter someone else's square.

→ 1 v 1 games on courts divided by a net.

→ You may not move with the ball/shuttle in hand.

Try to ... be aware of how you use a variety of different shots.

> **From where did you score most often? Why?**

> **How did speed, distance and height affect your game? Give one example.**

> **How did you discover your opponent's strengths and weaknesses?**

Game play

Focus: Giving your partner effective feedback on their performance in a game.

The game:

→ A short 1 v 1 or 2 v 2 game.

→ You observe your partner playing the game. In the table below, tick the **P/E (present/ effective)** box every time your partner makes a useful shot choice/placement/ recovery position. Tick **A/I (absent/inappropriate)** whenever you see them make a poor or no shot choice/placement/recovery position.

→ Then swap to allow your partner to observe your game.

Try to ... use shots that give your opponent less time to recover.

Shooting and Recovery Feedback Form					
Observer name:			Date: ☐ ☐ ☐ ☐ ☐ ☐		
Shot choice		**Shot placement**		**Recovery position**	
P/E	A/I	P/E	A/I	P/E	A/I

Now let's pick out two stars and a wish.

→ **Two stars:** Two things that went well.

→ **A wish:** One thing they could do differently to improve their game and delivery next time.

Defending an attack

Think about:

→ Returning shot – block, dig, close to net   → Cover and formations.

Watch this video and answer the questions below.

Go to YouTube and search for 'Top 20 Crazy Actions Beach Volleyball | 3rd Meter Spike | Best Block | Best Dig | Best Defense' (5:35).

Block		
Mark where the player blocking the shot stands (X) and where the player covering stands (0).		
Is that a good position? Why/why not?		
Dig		
Did the dig go forwards, backwards, upwards? Why?		
Was the dig high or low? Why?		
Close to the net		
What is the benefit of playing close to the net?		

Now watch this video and answer the questions below.

Go to YouTube and search for 'When Defense overcomes Attack' (7:16).

Cover and formations		
How did players move to cover each other? Give an example.		
Draw what formation they started in (X) and the shape they changed to (0).		
Why do you think they did this?		
Do you think supporters have an impact on the game and the players' performance?		

Winner stays on

Focus: *React* and *Respond* to an attack by using a variety of returning shots and being aware of your positioning.

The game:

→ 2 v 2. The players play a rally.

→ The winners stay on and the losers join the back of the queue and wait to try again.

→ The next two in the queue serve against the winners and play begins again.

Formations:

→ You and your teammate decide how you will divide the court and which section each of you will take.

Try to ... position yourself near the net to get a block.

Reflection 1

Defence preview/review	
How do you/did you prevent scoring?	
What tactics do you/did you use to give yourself more time to recover?	
How do you/did you deny the offence certain shots?	
How do you/did you work together?	

Reflection 2

How would you rate your performance of the following skills in defence? In the table below, score each element as follows:

1 Limited, rarely seen and ineffective.

2 Acceptable, seen most of the time, effective.

3 Very good, seen nearly all the time, very effective.

4 Excellent, seen all the time, extremely effective.

Defence skills analysis		
Skills and tactics	**Score**	**My target for improvement**
Positioning		
Communication		
Varied placement of shots		
Moving my opponent		
Footwork		

Divided court games feedback form

Using the rating scale below, select a number of stars from 1 to 5 to indicate your opinion: 5 = very strong; 3 = moderate; 1 = weak.

Observer name:	Review date: ☐☐ ☐☐ ☐☐
Success factor	**Your rating**
Can see the 4Rs (Read, Respond, React, Recover)	☆ ☆ ☆ ☆ ☆
Positioned well to create and deny space	☆ ☆ ☆ ☆ ☆
Shot to create space and move player	☆ ☆ ☆ ☆ ☆
Varied shots and placement	☆ ☆ ☆ ☆ ☆

Anticipated shot and moved to space	☆ ☆ ☆ ☆ ☆
Stayed in formation	☆ ☆ ☆ ☆ ☆
Chose the appropriate return shot	☆ ☆ ☆ ☆ ☆
Covered area or player	☆ ☆ ☆ ☆ ☆
Returned to recovery position after shot	☆ ☆ ☆ ☆ ☆

What do you need to improve on for the next game ...

In offence?

_____

_____

In defence?

_____

_____

What are you doing well ...

As a player?

_____

_____

As part of your team?

_____

_____

Making Clever Decisions: Tactical Awareness

> **LO 2.5** Respond, individually and as part of a team, to different games' scenarios.

In the course of a game, a whole range of situations arise to which you have to react and respond in the moment. In this section we'll examine some of these situations and consider the thinking behind your decisions. The scenarios call on you to apply the strategies, tactics and skills you have learned in your games units.

Making a decision in response to a given game situation is not a straightforward exercise. Many things will influence your thinking.

Rate the following in terms of the impact each has on your decision-making. Use the following grading system:

1 = Low	2 = Low to moderate	3 = Moderate
4 = Moderate to high	5 = High	

The situation that is presented		Individual influencers in our team	
My own strengths and weaknesses		The weather conditions	
My opponent's strengths and weaknesses		Everybody having a say	
The mix of ability in our team		The referee	

Scenarios

Here are a few scenarios to get you started. You can plan a tactical solution and play the game scenario for real, to see how it improves your performance.

Invasion games: positioning in defence

This game has been frozen at a 3 v 3 scenario. **Team 0 are attacking, team X are defending**. Team 0 are in strong offensive positions. Draw a line to indicate where defence players should move to counter the threat from team 0. Player 01 is in possession of the ball.

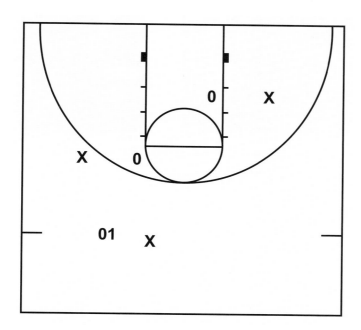

Is the attacking position a strong one? Explain.

1 _____

2 _____

3 _____

How is the new defence position more effective?

1 _____

2 _____

3 _____

Divided court games: creating space in opponent's court

In a singles match this divided court game has been frozen with the shuttle/ball being played to player B. Player B must now play a return.

→ Draw a dotted line to indicate where that shot should go.

→ Identify the stroke and why you have chosen it.

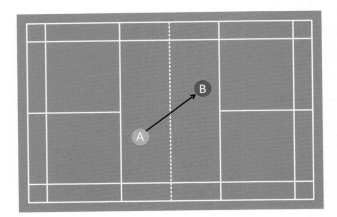

My chosen stroke: _____

Why it is appropriate:

❶ _____

❷ _____

❸ _____

Striking and fielding games: ball placement

This game has been frozen in time. It is your turn to bat. Your team needs a rounder to win and a half to draw the match. The field is set up as you see it. Draw a dotted line to indicate where you would hit the ball. The field is set up as you see it. You have a player at 2nd Base.

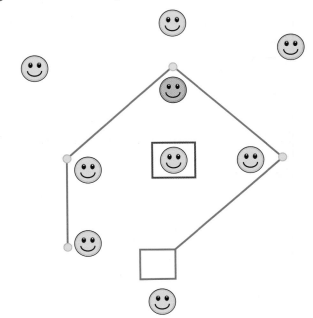

My chosen strike line	
Why I chose it	**1** _____ **2** _____ **3** _____

When deciding on your solution to the scenario, the following problem-solving approach might be useful:

What have we learned?

Let's do it!

Who's doing what?

What is the best and safest way for us?

How many ways can we respond?

What exactly is the challenge?

Let's follow these steps in deciding on a strategy in response to the following scenario.

Invasion games: Gaelic football

2 minutes left

1 point up

Your team **has possession** on your defence 40 m line.

What strategies and tactics do you use?

165

Team in possession

What is the challenge?	We have to keep possession and not let the other team get possession and score.
How many ways can we respond?	(a) Run down the clock. Create space, only make high-percentage passes, move to provide support and passing options. (b) Attack and score. (c) Bring everyone back and crowd the defence.
What is the best and safest way?	Option (a). Our strengths are in our fitness and movement on the pitch. The opposition defence is tight, strong down the centre and not as mobile. Option (b) risks losing possession in attack. In option (c), crowding the defence would draw the other team forward and run the risk of us fouling or losing the ball.
Who's doing what?	Wing players – cut in and out and hug the wings. Keep changing the ball carrier. Goalkeeper – provide feedback, instructions.
Let's do it!	Run the game beginning with possession from the centre circle.
What have we learned to take into our next challenge?	How did we: • create the open space? • move the ball? • implement the plan?

Team not in possession

What is the challenge?	We have to win back possession and score.
How many ways can we respond?	(a) Full press on the restart – intercept or win the first pass. (b) Chase the ball carrier. (c) Attack and score. Get the ball to our best scorer in a scoring position.
What is the best and safest way?	Our strengths are in our physical presence. We don't have the fitness to chase the ball carrier. Option (a) is best as time and the score are against us. We must reduce the opposition time and space on re-start. Force the opposition to: foul the ball; overcarry; make passes under pressure. Look to intercept or double tag a ball carrier. Get the ball to X to shoot at goal or draw the foul.
Who's doing what?	All players – pressure the re-start; close off the line between the ball and the support player; anticipate and win break-down. Captain calls the step-up. Goalkeeper – provides feedback on offence positions.

Let's do it!	Run the game beginning with possession from the centre circle.
What have we learned to take into our next challenge?	How did we: • close down the open space? • slow the ball? • implement the plan?

Your game scenario

Here is a blank form for you to respond to a scenario which you or your teacher would like to set as a challenge. Work out a plan of action and then play that scenario for real. Reflect on the effectiveness of your performance as a team and as an individual.

What is the challenge?	
How many ways can we respond?	❶ ❷ ❸
What is the best and safest way? Why?	
Who's doing what?	
Let's do it!	
What have we learned to take us into our next challenge?	

Taking a Look at Your Experience

 I wonder How did the Irish women's hockey team, ranked 12 out of 12, get to the World Cup final?

My thoughts: _____

_____

Reflection

In this strand:

I learned: _____

_____

_____

_____

I enjoyed: _____

_____

_____

_____

I would like to do more: _____

_____

_____

_____

My classmates helped me to learn when they ...

I did not enjoy:

Because:

Other comments:

The CBA

There are five aspects to the assessment of performance in games:

→ The range of skills and strategies used in responding to the attacking and defending scenario

→ The ability to respond effectively under pressure as an individual and as part of a team, where relevant

→ Evidence of creativity in the responses

→ An understanding of and adherence to the rules of the selected game

→ An ability to reflect on their overall learning in the strand.

The PE teacher, in consultation with the students, sets up modified game scenarios towards the end of the strand where students can demonstrate movement skills and strategies being used creatively and effectively in attacking and defending situations. Students are assessed on their individual play and the extent to which they contribute effectively to the team's response where this is relevant.

Alternatively, students could be required to gather video evidence of their performance in these modified game scenarios. Students could then submit a short clip demonstrating their performance in both attacking and defending. On completing their performance assessment in *Games*, students are required to reflect on their overall learning in this strand.

Assessment features of quality

Exceptional:

→ The performance includes an excellent range of skills and strategies executed competently, consistently and safely.

→ The student demonstrates an excellent ability to respond creatively under pressure, as an individual and as part of a team.

→ The student demonstrates a thorough understanding of and adherence to the rules and safety considerations in the selected game.

→ The student's reflection is of excellent quality.

Above expectations:

→ The performance includes a very good range of skills and strategies executed competently, consistently and safely.

→ The student demonstrates a very good ability to respond creatively under pressure, as an individual and as part of a team.

→ The student demonstrates a very good understanding of and adherence to the rules and safety considerations in the selected game.

→ The student's reflection is of very good quality.

In line with expectations:

→ The performance includes an acceptable range of skills and strategies executed competently, consistently and safely.

→ The student demonstrates some ability to respond creatively under pressure, as an individual and as part of a team.

→ The student demonstrates a good understanding of and adherence to the rules and safety considerations in the selected game.

→ The student's refection is of reasonable quality.

Yet to meet expectations:

→ The performance demonstrates limited skills and few strategies.

→ The student seldom responds effectively as an individual or as part of a team.

→ The student demonstrates an inadequate understanding of and adherence to the rules and safety considerations in the selected game.

→ The student's refection is limited.

CBA Reflection Form – Games

Consider using some of these words in your reflection:

Word Bank				
options	create space	position	width	depth
strategy	support	targeted	attack	defence
pressurise	organised	person-to-person	zone	angle of attack
advantage	service	anticipate	formation	

Attack

Which game category did you select?

Invasion ☐   Striking and fielding ☐   Divided court ☐

What was the attacking scenario you were presented with?

In how many ways could you respond to it as a team?

What was it about the opposition that influenced your decision?

Which strategy did you decide to adopt and why?

What was your role, as part of the team, in the strategy?

How did the strategy play out?

What skills did you demonstrate?

How consistent were you?

If the game plan broke down, how did you adapt?

How did the rules and safety considerations of the game influence your decisions?

Defence

What was the defending scenario you were presented with?

In how many ways could you respond to it as a team?

What was it about the opposition that influenced your decision?

Which strategy did you decide to adopt and why?

What was your role, as part of the team, in the strategy?

How did the strategy play out?

What skills did you demonstrate?

_____

_____

How consistent were you?

_____

_____

If the game plan broke down, how did you adapt?

_____

_____

How did the rules and safety considerations of the game influence your decisions?

_____

_____

Reflection Review Checklist

● I named the scenario (attack/defence).	
● I identified the options available to us and our choice of strategy.	
● I identified a number of skills and points in play where I demonstrated them.	
● I rated my consistency in the skills execution.	
● I explained how my performance was creative (e.g. creating space, depth, penetrating defence, responding to shots, etc.).	
● I explained my individual contribution to the performance (e.g. as first defender, forward/back, target, wing, service, captain).	
● My reflection is an honest judgement of my performance (not just a listing or description; I recognise my limitations and strengths).	
● I have used accurate games terms in my account.	
● I have explained how I complied with the rules and safety considerations of the game.	

Signature: _____

Date: _____

STRAND 3

Individual and Team Challenges

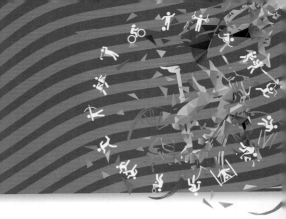

STRAND 3

Athletics

Looking at it ☐ Working on it ☐ Nailed it ☐

Athletics is one of the oldest organised sports in the world. Ireland even had its own athletics events, the Tailteann Games, which can be traced back to 632 BC. The most well-known competition is the Olympic Games, which started in Athens in 776 BC and included events like sprinting, wrestling and long jump. The athletics events at the modern Olympics involve three main skills – running, jumping and throwing – and sometimes all three together.

In this unit you will see if you have what it takes to become an Olympian. Take the torch and run with it!

 I wonder Does the shape of your body make you better at certain athletic events?

My thoughts: _____

_____

At the end of this unit I will be able to:

Learning Outcomes Strand 3: Athletics		Year 1	Year 2	Year 3
3.7	Perform competently, confidently and safely in a range of athletics events			
3.8	Demonstrate activities to enhance performance in athletic events, including physical and mental preparation			
3.9	Take responsibility for improving my own performance, based on personal strengths and developmental needs			

176

Class Challenge:

My Personal Challenge:

Athletics terminology

Competent	Doing something effectively or skilfully.
Recovery	Returning back to the normal position.
Acceleration	Rate at which you gain speed.
Drive	To move with a lot of power.
Stance	The way a person stands; their posture.
Rotational	Moving in a circular direction around one central point.
Approach	Come near or come closer to something from a distance.
Explosive	To use energy suddenly and forcefully.

Go to YouTube and search for:

Track Events:
'Track Events' (5:07).

Heptathlon: 'Johnson-Thompson wins Heptathlon Gold | World Athletics Championships 2019 | Doha Moments' (1:32).

Field Events: 'Men's and Women's Athletics Fields Events - Singapore 2010 Youth Games' (2:14).

Decathlon: 'Best of Ashton Eaton US Olympic Decathlon | Athlete Highlights' (10:37).

Athletics Events

Can you name these athletics events?

A		B		C	
D		E		F	

These athletics events are based on three *fundamental movement skills*.

Can you identify what they are?

1 _____

2 _____

3 _____

- Mental
- Physical

Preparation

Track events: Running

- Sprint
- Middle distance
- Long distance
- Relay

- High jump
- Long jump

Field events: Jumping

Field events: Throwing

- Javelin
- Shot put

Track Events: Running
Sprint

Take a guess …

What is the current world record time for the 100 m sprint?

Women: _____   Men: _____

Go to YouTube and search for:

Women: 'W 100m - Florence Griffith-Joyner' (1:38).

Men: 'Usain Bolt new 100m world record' (9:30).

Watch this video and write down five elements of the sprinters' running technique.

Go to YouTube and search for 'Sprint Form Slow Motion' (1:49).

1 _____

2 _____

3 _____

4 _____

5 _____

i   Ireland's Jason Smyth, a visually impaired athlete, is the fastest Paralympian in the world.

Safety first!

LO 3.7 Perform competently, confidently and safely in a range of athletics events.

1 Warm up properly before competing.

2 Don't use walls or fences to slow yourself down. Slow down before you get there.

3 Stay in your own lane.

4 Wear appropriate clothing and stay hydrated.

Why are these rules important? What will they help avoid?

_____

_____

_____

_____

Physical preparation

LO 3.8 Demonstrate activities to enhance performance in athletic events, including physical and mental preparation.

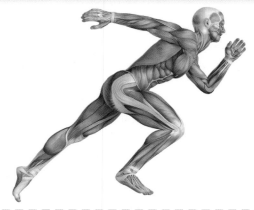

Which muscles do you use in sprinting?

1 _____

2 _____

3 _____

4 _____

With your partner, think of some activities that could get those muscles ready to run.
Write or draw your ideas in the table. Explain your choice.

Name:	Name:
Activities	Activities
Explanation	Explanation

Sprint from standing

In this activity, you and your partner are going to try sprinting following these directions.
Discuss with your partner and record what you noticed.

Try this …	What did you notice?
Keep your legs completely straight	
Don't move your arms from your side	
Lean forward as far as you can	
Plant your feet flat on the ground	

Now let's look at the correct running technique.

1 Keep your shoulders loose and your back straight.

2 Pretend that a string is pulling you up from your hips through your head and look straight ahead.

3 Your arm motion should be like getting a sweet from your pocket.

4 Bring your knees up and lift your toes up to your shin.

5 Land on the ball of your foot and push hard off the ground.

6 Bring the heel of your foot up so that you nearly flick your buttock with it.

Watch out for some common mistakes:

→ Reaching too far in your stride.

→ Heels flicking up behind your body.

→ Arms swinging across your body.

Technique analysis

In this activity, you and your partner are going to watch/video each other running, focusing on each other's technique. You will then analyse your own and your partner's performance to help you both improve.

In the table on page 183 write the relevant letter for each technique:

R = Rarely   **M =** Mostly   **A** = All the time

Technique				Attempt 1	Attempt 2	Attempt 3
Swing		Driving the foot down and picking it up quickly	Me			
			My partner			
		Landing on the balls of your feet, heel not touching the ground	Me			
			My partner			
Support		Keeping the body upright and stable	Me			
			My partner			
		Keeping the shoulders loose	Me			
			My partner			
		Bringing the heel up, nearly flicking the buttock	Me			
			My partner			
Drive		Relaxed motion of arms from hip to eye level	Me			
			My partner			
		Knees are lifted and hips are high	Me			
			My partner			
		Toe raised towards shin	Me			
			My partner			
Recovery		Foot leaves the ground as quickly as possible	Me			
			My partner			
		Heel up, flicking buttock	Me			
			My partner			

Now give your partner some feedback:

→ Your sprint was good because you _____ . It would be better if you _____ .

→ One part of your technique that was good was _____ . What would make it even better is _____ .

→ _____ worked well. Next time, if you _____ it will be better.

And analyse your own performance:

I improved from attempt 1 to attempt 3 by ...

Sprint from start position

In this activity, you and your partner will add these steps to the techniques you have already tried. Listen to their feedback and/or watch back your performance and analyse it together. You can also time your sprint.

In the table below write the relevant letter for each technique:

R = Rarely   **M =** Mostly   **A** = All the time

Technique			Attempt 1	Attempt 2	Attempt 3
On your marks	Front foot is two lengths of your foot from the start line	Me			
		My partner			
	The knee of the back foot is ahead of the front foot	Me			
		My partner			
	Hands more than shoulder width apart	Me			
		My partner			
	Thumb and forefinger behind the line	Me			
		My partner			
Get set	Hips raised above shoulder height	Me			
		My partner			
	Shoulders in line with hands	Me			
		My partner			
	Front knee at 90° and back knee at 120–140°	Me			
		My partner			

Technique			Attempt 1	Attempt 2	Attempt 3
Go	Power off from both legs	Me			
		My partner			
	Drive arms backwards with force	Me			
		My partner			
	Drive the knee of back leg forward	Me			
		My partner			
	Straight line from the heel to the head	Me			
		My partner			
Accelerate	Body stays low at the start	Me			
		My partner			
	Arms drive forward	Me			
		My partner			
	Take increasingly long steps	Me			
		My partner			

I wonder Are you faster starting from a standing position or from the ground? Why?

My thoughts:

Relay

Take a guess …

What is the current world record for the 4 x 100 m relay?

Women: _____   Men: _____

Go to YouTube and search for:

Women: 'USA Break Women's 4 x 100m Relay World Record – London 2012 Olympics' (7:13).

Men: 'Jamaica Break Men's 4x100m World Record – London 2012 Olympics' (18:20).

185

Ireland's women's relay team – Molly Scott, Gina Akpe-Moses, Patience Jumbo-Gula and Ciara Neville – won silver in the 4 x 100 m relay at the 2018 IAAF World U20 Championships.

Watch this video and make notes on the baton exchange. Don't worry about the commentary.

Go to YouTube and search for 'WR 4x100m 37.10 Relay Men - slow motion [HQ]' (1:22).

1 _____

2 _____

3 _____

4 _____

5 _____

Exchange zone

Sprint   Exchange   Sprint

In this activity, you will work in a group of four to practise your baton exchange. Two will practise the exchange and two will observe. Then switch.

There will be a designated space – exchange zone – laid out for you in the middle of the hall/pitch. You can only pass the baton in this space.

In the table on page 187 write the relevant letter for each technique for each person (A, B, C and D):

R = Rarely   **M** = Mostly   **A** = All the time

Technique		Attempt 1	Attempt 2	Attempt 3
Passing the baton				
	Stretch out arm, place the top of the baton in the palm of partner's open hand			
	Shout 'Hand' to let partner know when to extend their arm			
Receiving the baton				
	Stretch receiving arm out straight behind you at shoulder height			
	Palm open and thumb pointing at the ground			
	Arm is kept still until the baton is placed in the palm			
	Keep looking ahead – don't turn around or break your stride			

What was challenging? How did you overcome that challenge?

Now practise your technique in a full relay!

I wonder Why do the runners in the first lane start further back than the runners in the eighth lane?

187

Our relay team

3rd Runner
Name:

Leg	Baton skills	Athletic strengths
3	Receives and passes the baton	• Takes off quickly • Stays in their lane when running the curve

2nd Runner
Name:

Leg	Baton skills	Athletic strengths
2	Receives and passes the baton	• Fast runner • Maintains a fast pace • Very good endurance

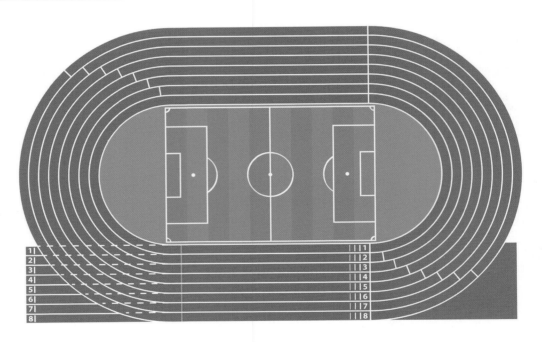

4th Runner
Name:

Leg	Baton skills	Athletic strengths
4	Receives the baton	• The fastest and most driven runner • Can overtake other runners

1st Runner
Name:

Leg	Baton skills	Athletic strengths
1	Passes the baton	• Accelerates quickly • Good balance • Stays in their lane when running the curve

Reflection

➜ Why did you pick your runners in that order?

➜ Was your baton exchange good? How do you know?

➜ If you were to run that race again, how would you change it?

Field Events: Throwing

Javelin

Take a guess …

What is the current world record in the javelin?

Women: _____   Men: _____

Go to YouTube and search for:

Women: 'Barbora Spotakova / Sets World Record / Women's Javelin Throw' (1:17).

Men: 'Jan Zelezny world record Javelin' (1:05).

At the age of 19, Keshorn Walcott from Trinidad and Tobago became the youngest person ever to win an Olympic gold medal in javelin.

Watch this video and note down five aspects of the javelin thrower's technique.

Go to YouTube and search for 'Thomas Röhler - The Compilation' (3:01).

1 _____

2 _____

3 _____

4 _____

5 _____

Safety first!

> **LO 3.7** Perform competently, confidently and safely in a range of athletics events.

1 Warm up properly before competing.

2 Do not throw until the teacher calls 'Throw'.

3 Only collect when the teacher/official says 'Collect'.

4 Only throw into the boundary and only when it's clear.

5 Carry the javelin point down when you walk back to the starting position.

6 Walk, never run, with a javelin in hand.

Rules:

➡ You cannot step over the throwing line.

➡ Your throw is disallowed if the javelin lands outside the boundary.

> **Why are these rules important? What will they help avoid?**
>
> _____
>
> _____

Physical preparation

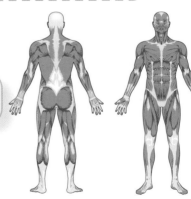

> **LO 3.8** Demonstrate activities to enhance performance in athletic events, including physical and mental preparation.

> **What muscles do you use in the javelin?**
>
> **1** _____
>
> **2** _____
>
> **3** _____
>
> **4** _____

With your partner, think of some activities that could get those muscles ready to throw. Write or draw your ideas in the table. Explain your choice.

Name:	Name:
Activities	Activities
Explanation	Explanation

Pull and whip

LO 3.9 Take responsibility for improving their own performance based on personal strengths and developmental needs.

In this activity you are going to 'pull and whip' a heavy ball forwards. Try to copy the movements you saw in the video on page 190.

Get thinking and talk to your partner:

How are you using your **body** as you pull and whip the ball?			Why is it effective?
	Lean forwards	☐	
	Lean backwards	☐	
	Stand up straight	☐	
	Curl over	☐	
	Stand sideways	☐	
	Face forwards	☐	

How are you using your **arms** as you pull and whip the ball?		Why is it effective?
	Arm bent ☐	
	Arm straight ☐	
	Arm above shoulder ☐	
	Arm at shoulder level ☐	
	Whipping motion ☐	
	Throwing motion ☐	
	Opposite arm in front ☐	
	Opposite arm at the side ☐	

How are you using your **legs** as you pull and whip the ball?		Why is it effective?
	Feet together ☐	
	Feet shoulder-width apart ☐	
	Feet pointing forward ☐	
	Feet pointing to the side ☐	
	Feet move first ☐	
	Arms move first ☐	
	Hips move first ☐	

Javelin grip

How will you hold the javelin?

Try these grips and see what feels most comfortable. Make sure your grip is firm but relaxed.

American grip	Finnish grip	V grip
The thumb and first finger are around the rim of the cord on the javelin.	The thumb and second finger are around the rim off the cord on the javelin. The first finger is supporting the shaft of the javelin.	The javelin is held between the first and second finger around the rim of the cord.

Standing throw

Basic technique:

1 Arm straight back behind you at shoulder level.

2 Javelin in the palm of your hand.

3 Body facing side-on with feet shoulder-width apart. Front and back feet facing forward.

4 Start throw by swinging on to back foot and moving forward.

5 Elbow above your shoulder as you pull and whip the javelin.

6 Hips lead before arms.

Give it a go! But watch out for some common mistakes:

→ Hips turning after the arms.

→ Elbow not above shoulder level.

→ Not transferring weight from back to front foot.

Now give your partner some feedback:

→ Your throw was good because you _____. It would be better if you _____.

→ One part of your technique that was good was _____. What will make it even better is _____.

→ _____ worked well. Next time, if you _____ it will be better.

Technique analysis

In this activity, you and your partner will pull and whip the javelin following the technique on page 195. Observe/video each other and give each other feedback. Aim to improve your performance over three attempts.

R = Rarely   **M =** Mostly   **A** = All the time

Technique			Attempt 1	Attempt 2	Attempt 3
Grip	Javelin resting in the palm of the hand	Me			
		My partner			
	One of the three grips used	Me			
		My partner			
	Arm extended straight back and parallel to the ground. Tip of the javelin at eye level	Me			
		My partner			
Stance	Standing side-on with feet shoulder-width apart	Me			
		My partner			
	Non-dominant foot in front, facing the direction of the throw	Me			
		My partner			
	Dominant foot behind at one o'clock	Me			
		My partner			
	Weight on the back leg	Me			
		My partner			
Transfer of weight and delivery	Move weight to back leg and then move forwards	Me			
		My partner			
	Straighten back leg and drive through hips before arms move	Me			
		My partner			
	Elbow stays above the shoulder when throwing	Me			
		My partner			
	Body is tall and javelin is released at 45 degrees	Me			
		My partner			

What did you find most challenging? How did you overcome that challenge?

Shot put

Take a guess …

What is the current world record in the shot put?

Women: _____   Men: _____

Go to YouTube and search for:

Women: 'World Track & Field 1991 Shot Put Women Natalya Lisovskaya' (1:00).

Men: 'Ryan Crouser wins Shot Put gold with an Olympic Record' (1:35).

 Victor Costello is the only Irishman to have competed at the Olympics and in the Six Nations. He qualified for the Olympics in Barcelona in the shot put and has 39 Ireland caps to his name.

Watch this video and note down five aspects of the shot putter's technique.

Go to YouTube and search for 'Shot put - Ryan Crouser Olympic record SLO-MO video' (0:58).

1 _____

2 _____

3 _____

4 _____

5 _____

Safety first!

LO 3.7 Perform competently, confidently and safely in a range of athletics events.

SAFETY FIRST

1. Warm up properly before competing.
2. Use the weight that is appropriate for your age.
3. Only throw when the official calls 'Throw'.
4. Only collect when the official says 'Collect'.
5. Only throw into the boundary and only when it's clear.
6. Collect the shot and carry it back to the throwing circle.

Rules:

→ You cannot step over or on the stopboard.

→ The shot must be close to or touching the neck.

→ Your throw is disallowed if it lands outside the boundary.

→ You must walk out of the back of the half circle after the shot has landed.

Why are these rules important? What will they help avoid?

_____

_____

_____

Physical preparation

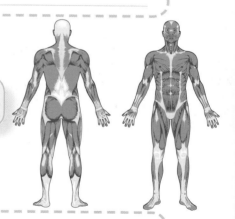

LO 3.8 Demonstrate activities to enhance performance in athletic events, including physical and mental preparation.

What muscles do you use in the shot put?

❶ _____

❷ _____

❸ _____

❹ _____

With your partner, think of some activities that could get those muscles ready to throw. Write or draw your ideas in the table. Explain your choice.

Name:	Name:
Activities	Activities
Explanation	Explanation

Grip

Go to YouTube and search for 'How to Put a Shot ft. Reese Hoffa | Olympians' Tips' (3:22).

What it should look like:

→ Shot held at the bottom of the fingers, **not** in the palm!

→ Thumb and little finger on either side of the shot.

Standing throw – basic technique

1. Hold shot against your neck – 'clean palm, dirty neck'.

2. Little finger to your ear, thumb to your collar bone.

3 Keep your elbow up and parallel to the ground.

4 Stand side-on with knees bent. Weight on the back leg.

5 Chin, knee, toe in line.

6 Drive hips forward and push throw low to high. Punchout!

7 Finish with hips facing forward and straight arm – wave goodbye.

Give it a go! But watch out for some common mistakes:

→ Low elbow throughout.

→ Removing shot from the neck.

→ Throwing across the body instead of turning forwards.

→ Not driving the hip forward.

Technique analysis

LO 3.9 Take responsibility for improving my own performance.

In this activity, you and your partner will follow the technique below. Observe/video each other and give each other feedback. Aim to improve your performance over three attempts.

R = Rarely   **M =** Mostly   **A** = All the time

Technique			Attempt 1	Attempt 2	Attempt 3
Power stance	Chin, knee, toe	Me			
		My partner			
	Elbow parallel to the ground	Me			
		My partner			
	Shot against the neck	Me			
		My partner			
	Back to the direction of the throw	Me			
		My partner			
Transfer of weight	Powers off back leg	Me			
		My partner			
	Weight moves to front leg	Me			
		My partner			
	Elbow stays high	Me			
		My partner			
	Low to high movement	Me			
		My partner			
Delivery and release	Arm high and straight	Me			
		My partner			
	Straight elbow and wrist-punchout!	Me			
		My partner			
	Drives hip forward Swings non-throwing arm back	Me			
		My partner			

What did you find most challenging? How did you overcome that challenge?

Practise with a partner – using technology if available – and give each other feedback:

→ Your throw was good because you _____. It would be

better if you _____.

→ One part of your technique that was good was _____.

What will make it even better is _____.

→ _____ worked well. Next time, if you _____

_____ it will be better.

Reflection
Javelin and shot put

Which throw would you perform at a competition – javelin or shot put? Why?

What are the benefits of the glide/rotation and slide/run up over the standing throw?

What was the most challenging part of the javelin and shot put? How did you overcome that challenge?

What were you strongest at when performing the javelin and shot put? Why?

Field Events: Jumping
High jump

Take a guess ...

What is the current high jump world record?

Women: _____   Men: _____

Go to YouTube and search for:

Women: 'Stefka Kostadinova World High Jump Record at World Chapionships in Rome 1987' (2:22).

Men: Javier Sotomayor - High Jump World Record' (4:51).

 Adrian O'Dwyer holds the Irish high jump record – 2.3 m. He represented Ireland at the Olympics in 2004.

Watch this video and note down five aspects of the high jumper's technique.

Go to YouTube and search for 'The best of Gianmarco Tamberi - High Jump' (6:33).

1 _____

2 _____

3 _____

4 _____

5 _____

Safety first!

1 Warm up properly before competing.

2 Only jump when the landing mat is clear.

3 Make sure the landing mat is secure.

4 Make sure the ground is not slippery.

5 Check there are no loose stones on the run up.

Rules:

→ You must take off on one foot.

→ You will be eliminated after three consecutive failed attempts. You must complete a trial within 1 minute of being called.

→ A jump is successful if the bar stays in place.

Why are these rules important? What will they help avoid?

Physical preparation

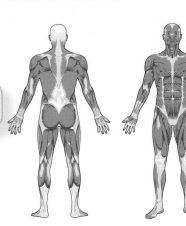

LO 3.8 Demonstrate activities to enhance performance in athletic events, including physical and mental preparation.

What muscles do you use in the high jump?

1

2

3

4

With your partner, think of some activities that could get those muscles ready to jump.
Write or draw your ideas in the table. Explain your choice.

Name:	Name:
Activities	Activities
Explanation	Explanation

Fosbury flop

LO 3.7 Perform competently, confidently and safely.

Go to YouTube and search for 'How One Man Changed the High Jump Forever | The Olympics on the Record' (4:24).

| Approach | Take off | Flight | Landing |

Approach:

1 Run towards the bar at a 'J'.

2 Lean in at the curve.

Take off:

3 Body is straight and tall.

4 Plant the outside leg and drive the inside knee up.

Flight:

5 Inside arm reaches up and over the bar.

6 Hips drive up and back arches.

Landing:

7 Land on your shoulders and back; kick legs up.

8 Keep head close to chest.

Give it a go! But watch out for some common mistakes:

→ Slowing down when approaching the bar.

→ Taking off too far out from the bar.

→ Arriving at the bar on the wrong take-off leg.

Practise with a partner and give each other feedback:

→ Your jump was good because you _____. It would be

better if you _____.

→ One part of your technique that was good was _____.

What will make it even better is _____.

→ _____ worked well. Next time, if you _____

_____ it will be better.

Technique analysis

In this activity, you and your partner will follow the technique on page 207. Observe/video each other and give each other feedback. Aim to improve your performance over three attempts.

R = Rarely   **M** = Mostly   **A** = All the time

Technique			Attempt 1	Attempt 2	Attempt 3
Approach	Upright run on approach	Me			
		My partner			
	Lean at ankles into the curve	Me			
		My partner			
	Take-off foot pointing at landing mat	Me			
		My partner			
Take Off	Outside leg plants, driving body straight up	Me			
		My partner			
	Knee of inside leg is driven upwards to 90 degrees	Me			
		My partner			
	Straighten hip, knee and ankle	Me			
		My partner			
Flight	Inside arm reaches across and over the bar	Me			
		My partner			
	Hips are pushed up and back is arched	Me			
		My partner			
	Knees are apart	Me			
		My partner			
Landing	Head to chest	Me			
		My partner			
	Landing on shoulders and back with legs in the air	Me			
		My partner			

What did you find most challenging? How did you overcome that challenge?

Long jump

Take a guess ...

What is the current long jump world record?

Women: _____   Men: _____

Go to YouTube and search for:

Women: 'Chistyakova Salto de Longitud Femenino (1988)' (0:41).

Men: 'World Record Long Jump of 8.95 metres' (1:44).

Watch this video and note down five aspects of the long jumper's technique.

Peter O'Connor, a Wicklow man, held the world record in the long jump – 7.3 m – for 20 years, and he held the Irish record for 90 years.

Go to YouTube and search for 'Men's long jump in slow motion' (1:58).

1 _____

2 _____

3 _____

4 _____

5 _____

Safety first!

1 Warm up properly before competing.

2 Only jump when the area is clear.

3 Make sure the area is free from any objects.

4 Make sure the sand is soft and raked.

5 Bend knees on landing to absorb impact.

Rules:

→ You must take off on one foot.

→ You get three opportunities to clear a distance before being knocked out.

→ If the foul line on the take-off board is touched, the jump is disallowed.

→ Your jump is measured from the foul line to the nearest place of contact in the sand.

Why are these rules important? What will they help avoid?

Physical preparation

LO 3.8 Demonstrate activities to enhance performance in athletic events, including physical and mental preparation.

What muscles do you use in the long jump?

1

2

3

4

With your partner, think of some activities that could get those muscles ready to jump. Write or draw your ideas in the table. Explain your choice.

Name:	Name:
Activities	Activities
Explanation	Explanation

Take-off and landing

In this activity you are going to jump from one leg to two legs. You will be jumping from a stationary position.

You will be given a cone. Place the cone at a distance that will challenge you and try to jump past it. Increase the distance when you're successful.

Keep in mind:

→ Stretch your arms high above your head to get height.

→ Land softly with bent knees and sit into your landing.

How many metres was your longest jump?

_____

What helped you achieve this distance?

_____

_____

Basic long jump technique

| Approach | Take-off | Flight/Hang | Landing |

Long jump basics: Go to YouTube and search for 'Brianna Glenn: Long Jump Basics' (3:51).

Approach:

1 Use a sprinting technique.

2 Gather speed approaching the board.

Take off:

3 Plant the take-off foot.

4 Drive down to fully extend take-off leg.

5 Swing free leg vigorously forwards and upwards.

6 Be as tall as possible on take-off.

Flight:

7 Body upright and take-off leg drawn upwards and forwards.

8 Both legs straightened for landing.

Landing:

9 Body bent forward.

10 Arms pulled back.

11 Land with heels first and soft knees.

Give it a go! But watch out for some common mistakes:

→ Slowing down when approaching the board.

→ Not driving upwards.

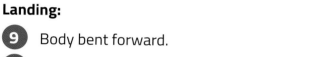

Practise with a partner and give each other feedback:

→ Your jump was good because you _____. It would be better if you _____.

→ One part of your technique that was good was _____. What will make it even better is _____.

→ _____ worked well. Next time, if you _____ _____ it will be better.

Technique analysis

LO 3.9 Take responsibility for improving their own performance.

In this activity, you and your partner will follow the technique below. Observe/video each other and give each other feedback. Aim to improve your performance over three attempts.

R = Rarely   **M** = Mostly   **A** = All the time

Technique			Attempt 1	Attempt 2	Attempt 3
Approach	Fast run-up using sprinting technique	Me			
		My partner			
	Does not slow down approaching board	Me			
		My partner			
	Looking up, not down at the board	Me			
		My partner			
Take Off	Takes off on one foot	Me			
		My partner			
	Drive down and back motion used on the planted foot	Me			
		My partner			
	Knee of free leg drives up and forwards	Me			
		My partner			
Flight	Holds free leg at 90 degrees through the air	Me			
		My partner			
	Body stays upright	Me			
		My partner			
	Legs move upwards and forwards, extending	Me			
		My partner			
Landing	Body bent forward, arms pulled back, legs straight	Me			
		My partner			
	Heels land first, softly, with bent knees	Me			
		My partner			

What did you find most challenging? How did you overcome that challenge?

Reflection
High Jump

Which jump would you perform at a competition – high jump or long jump? Why?

What were the most challenging technical parts of that jump?

What advice were you given by your partner? Did you agree with them? Why?

What were you strongest at when performing the high jump and long jump? Why?

Mental Preparation

LO 3.8 Demonstrate activities to enhance performance in athletic events, including physical and mental preparation.

Talent will get you to the starting blocks, but determination will get you to the finish line ...

Go to YouTube and search for 'Usain Bolt - Elements of a Champion | Gillette World Sport' (2:18).

How many Irish/Olympic athletics champions can you name?

_____

_____

Go to YouTube and search for:
'Usain Bolt new 100m world record' (9:30).

Find videos of Tyson Gay (USA) and Usain Bolt (Jamaica). Focus on what they do before they race. What do you think their mental preparation is?

Tyson Gay	Usain Bolt

IMAGERY   **ROUTINE**   **SELF-TALK**

Think about a time everything went right! Imagine that performance in your head

+

Create a routine that prepares you for competition

+

Pick three key phrases and repeat them to yourself. 'I can do this. Give it all you've got. Be strong'

=

Mental preparedness

My Athletic Profile

Imagine that you are an Olympic Athlete like Thomas Röhler. Fill in 'My Athletic Profile' below, selecting the country you represent and the event you qualified for. Undertake your three attempts and note your results in the Olympic Final.

My Athletic Profile

<table>
<tr><td rowspan="8" style="text-align:center;">Place image here</td><td>Name: _____</td><td></td><td></td></tr>
<tr><td>Country: _____</td><td></td><td></td></tr>
<tr><td>Flag:</td><td></td><td></td></tr>
<tr><td></td><td></td><td></td></tr>
<tr><td></td><td></td><td></td></tr>
<tr><td>Date of birth: _____</td><td></td><td></td></tr>
<tr><td>Event: _____</td><td></td><td></td></tr>
<tr><td>Medals: _____</td><td></td><td></td></tr>
</table>

Preparation

Physical	Mental		
Warm-up:	**Focus:**		
● Raise pulse rate ☐	● Imagery ☐		
● Flexibility ☐	● Routine ☐		
● Mental/movement rehearsal ☐	● Self-talk ☐		

Event: _____	Attempt 1	Attempt 2	Attempt 3
Time/Distance/Height			

Final result:

Ranking: _____	Performance: _____

215

The Athletics CBA

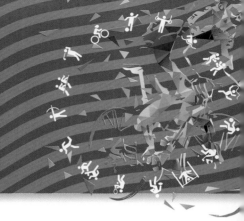

Students complete their performance assessment in one athletic event in a 'competitive' context, following the rules and safety regulations for the event. The student should be given at least two opportunities to demonstrate their best performance.

There are five aspects to the performance assessment in athletics:

→ Skill and technique in the selected athletic event performed under pressure

→ Ability to compete under pressure

→ Adherence to the rules of the event

→ Adherence to the safety precautions of the event

→ An ability to reflect on their overall learning in the strand.

Assessment features of quality

Exceptional:

→ The student demonstrates an excellent level of skill and technique.

→ The student demonstrates an excellent ability to compete effectively under pressure.

→ The student displays an excellent understanding of the rules of the event, including safety considerations.

→ The student's reflection is of excellent quality.

Above expectations:

→ The student demonstrates a very good level of skill and technique.

→ The student demonstrates a very good ability to compete effectively under pressure.

→ The student displays a very good understanding of the rules of the event, including safety considerations.

→ The student's reflection is of very good quality.

In line with expectations:

→ The student demonstrates a good level of skill and technique.

→ The student demonstrates a good ability to compete effectively under pressure.

→ The student displays a good understanding of the rules of the event, including safety considerations.

→ The student's reflection is of reasonable quality.

Yet to meet expectations:

→ The performance demonstrates very limited skill and technique.

→ The student demonstrates a very limited ability to compete under pressure.

→ The student displays an inadequate understanding of the rules of the event and safety considerations.

→ The student's reflection is of limited quality.

CBA Reflection Form – Athletics

Consider using some of these words in your reflection:

Word Bank			
explosive	accelerate	drive	approach
focused	mental	agility	rehearse
track	field	technique	athlete
skill	compete		

1 **What technical aspects of my performance in this athletic event was I pleased with and why?**

_____

_____

_____

2 **What parts of my performance in this athletic event was I less pleased with and why?**

_____

_____

_____

3 What did I do to comply with the rules and safety regulations of the event?

_____

_____

4 How did I demonstrate my focus and ability to compete under pressure?

_____

_____

5 What advice would I give to another student preparing for their performance assessment in athletics?

_____

_____

Reflection Review Checklist

I mentioned my event.	
Specific skills and techniques	
I described where I could and could not see the skills/techniques in my own performance.	
I explained what made my performance good.	
I used terms from my analysis.	
Competing under pressure	
I focused in all three attempts.	
I maintained good technique throughout.	
Rules and safety	
I identified the rules I followed.	
I explained where and how I kept safety in mind.	
My reflection	
My reflection is true to my performance.	
It recognises my strengths and limitations.	
It gives explanations, not just descriptions	

Signature: _____

Date: _____

Aquatics

Looking at it ☐   Working on it ☐   Nailed it ☐

Swimming is a lifelong skill that is healthy and fun. When you are confident in the water you can participate in many activities, from the recreational to the adventurous. Your 60 minutes of moderate to vigorous physical activity (MVPA) can be met just as well in swimming as in any other physical activity.

The swimming programme is designed to help you develop your swimming strokes, your confidence in the water, your awareness of personal safety around water, the possibilities for improving your fitness using water and your respect for water as a natural resource. There is an ocean of possibilities awaiting you!

 Swimming uses every muscle group in the body: core abdominal, lower back, shoulder, forearm, upper back, glutes, hamstring, and hip flexor muscles. Swimming burns more calories than running or biking.

 I wonder Who is more likely to float, a marathon runner or a sumo wrestler? Why?

My thoughts: _____

_____

At the end of this unit I will be able to:

Learning Outcomes Strand 3: Aquatics		Year 1	Year 2	Year 3
3.4	Perform competently and confidently in a range of swimming strokes			
3.5	Respond appropriately to a range of water safety scenarios			
3.6	Take responsibility for improving my own performance, based on personal strengths and developmental needs			

Class Challenge:

My Personal Challenge:

Front crawl common errors: Go to YouTube and search for 'Common Freestyle Mistakes in Swimming' (4:41).

50 pool exercises: Go to YouTube and search for '50 Pool Exercises | Choices Coach | Sara Moser' (12:41).

Aquatics terminology

HELP	Heat escape lessening position – reduces heat loss in cold water.
Streamlined	Being streamlined improves your movement in water. The less resistance you create, the easier your progress.
Stroke	Each style of swimming is called a stroke, e.g. breaststroke, backstroke, etc.
Aquafit	A term that describes many fitness activities that take place in water.
Survival swimming	The ability to stay afloat and alive in water.
Buoyancy	The ability of your body to float. Buoyancy will determine whether you float or sink in water.
Treading water	Keeping your mouth and nose above water by kicking the water downwards.
Hypothermia	Hypothermia occurs when your body gets so cold that it starts to shut down.

I wonder How does an efficient swimmer move in water?

1 _____

2 _____

3 _____

Do you recognise these swimming-related images? For each image, choose the correct letter from the grid below and write it in the right-hand columns.

Stroke/flag	Letter	Stroke/flag	Letter

A	Front crawl	E	Butterfly
B	Breaststroke	F	Backstroke
C	Dangerous water for swimming	G	Lifeguards patrol here
D	Watercraft in use – not safe to swim	H	Huddle

Which stroke is the fastest? _____

Which stroke is the most popular for recreational swimming? _____

In which stroke is your face most out of the water? _____

Ground Rules

It is important that you feel comfortable and safe when participating in swimming lessons. Let's consider how you might go about doing that.

With a partner, list your fears and hopes for the swimming programme. Record these in the appropriate column below.

Fears	Hopes

Now link up with another pair. Agree on three rules you think would help to make the lesson a safe and effective learning space while you are at the pool.

Our rules
1
2
3

Pool rules

You must also follow school rules and the rules of the pool facility. They may include some of the following.

Write in the box beside each point why it is important.

Rule	Why it is important
Swimwear should be suitable and reasonably tight-fitting	
Jewellery should not be taken to or worn in the pool	
Swimming hats should be worn	
Use shower and toilets before entering the pool	
Goggles are useful but you may be asked to remove them	
No running on the pool deck	
Do not enter the water until instructed to do so	
Obey the lifeguard's instructions and whistle	
Respect other pool users	
Respect pool equipment	

Safe Entry into the Water

Entry into the pool must be done safely. Before entering the pool, check which is the deep end and which is the shallow end. Entry into water other than in a pool demands more careful assessment. As you grow in confidence your range of options will expand to include more technical entries.

Use the criteria attached to each entry below and instruct your partner on how to enter the water correctly using that method. Alternatively, use the criteria to analyse your partner's entry and offer some helpful feedback.

Steps		
	Begin at the steps	
	Turn your back to the water	
	Place a hand on each rail	
	Step down and lower your body slowly into the water	
	Keep hold of the rails throughout	
Sitting swivel	Begin in sitting position with feet in the water	
	Place both hands to one side	
	Swivel to turn your back to the water	
	Lower your body slowly into the water	
	Keep hold of the poolside throughout	
Straddle jump	Straddle step forward into the water	
	Head high, chin up	
	Arms wide	
	Bring legs forcefully together on entry	
	Press arms to side	
Pencil	Step right out	
	Bring feet tight together on entry	
	Raise hands above head	
	On entry, open arms wide to reduce depth	
	Kick to surface	

Fill in the table below by selecting one of the options available in each column. Identify the best and safest conditions for each type of entry.

→ Is the water clear or unclear?

→ Is the water deep or shallow?

→ Is the water familiar or unfamiliar?

→ Is the water far below you or level with you?

→ Are you a confident swimmer or a beginner?

→ Are there other swimmers in the water?

Entering the water safely

	Clear/ unclear	Deep/ shallow	Known/ unknown	Far below/ level	Beginner/ confident	Busy/ quiet
Sitting swivel						
Steps						
Straddle						
Pencil						
Racing start						

Which entries are best if you need to keep your head above water?

Why could this be important in a life-saving situation?

How can you prevent water rushing up your nose?

Floating: Know Your Depth

Floating enables you to save a certain amount of energy, buying you time to assess your situation and regain your composure.

Holding on to the side of the pool (or free from the side if you are more confident), work out which body position helps you to float best.

My body position and why: _____

Pool depth

How do you measure up against the pool?

Stand by the water measure in the pool (e.g. 1 m : 1.5 m : 1.8 m). Note how high the water comes up your body. If you are in the deep end, can you pencil drop to touch the floor with your toes? How much deeper than you is the floor?

If you walk from the shallow end towards the deep end, at what point do you begin to lose your balance/control? Lie on your back and kick to get back to a safe place. Only do this task under the supervision of your teacher/swimming instructor.

I wonder Why do you begin to lose your balance in water?

1 _____
2 _____
3 _____

227

Standing up mid-swim

What helps you to stand up from lying on your front?

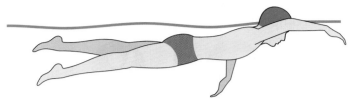

1 Lie on your front in the water.

2 Bring both knees towards your chest.

3 Pull the water back towards your feet with both hands at the same time.

4 Stand up straight.

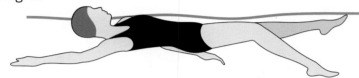

What helps you to stand up from lying on your back?

1 _____

2 _____

3 _____

Experiment with random pieces of everyday equipment as flotation devices – buckets, balls, empty two-litre milk cartons. (All items need to be clean and cleared for use by the pool authorities.) A flotation device could someday be the difference between someone sinking or staying afloat.

How effective are your items in helping you stay afloat? Tick the relevant column: A for Highly effective; B for Somewhat effective; C for Not effective.

Item		A	B	C
1				
2				
3				

Stroke Technique

LO 3.4 Perform competently and confidently in a range of swimming strokes.

 I wonder If you close your mouth, start humming and slowly sink below the water, what happens?

My thoughts: _____

_____

Swimming classes help you analyse and improve your stroke technique. A good technique will make your movement in water more efficient and more comfortable.

Read the descriptions of each stroke in the table below. Write the letter of each description in the box next to the picture it describes. Look closely at each image and the technique involved.

Front crawl		

A	Breathe in as head turns to the side.	D	Arm recovery is relaxed, with the elbow higher than the hand. Drag fingers over water surface.
B	Body lying on front, eyes looking forward and down.	E	Arm pushes back as head starts to turn in preparation for breathing.
C	Turn face back into the water and begin to breathe out.	F	Hand enters water just inside shoulder line. Pull down and back with elbow bent. Body rolls to side.

229

Backstroke

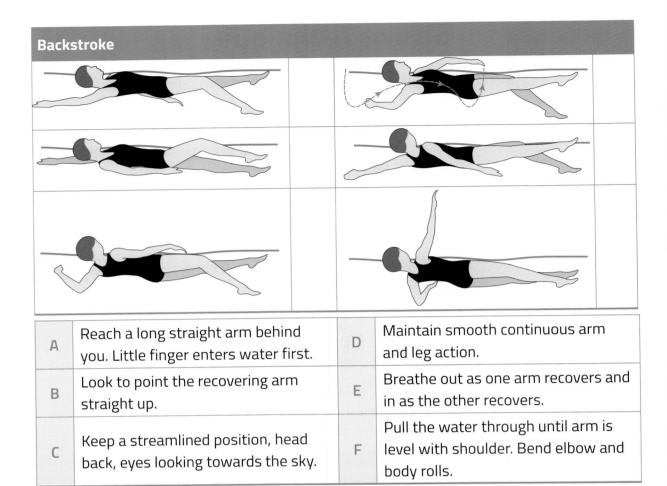

A	Reach a long straight arm behind you. Little finger enters water first.	D	Maintain smooth continuous arm and leg action.
B	Look to point the recovering arm straight up.	E	Breathe out as one arm recovers and in as the other recovers.
C	Keep a streamlined position, head back, eyes looking towards the sky.	F	Pull the water through until arm is level with shoulder. Bend elbow and body rolls.

Breaststroke

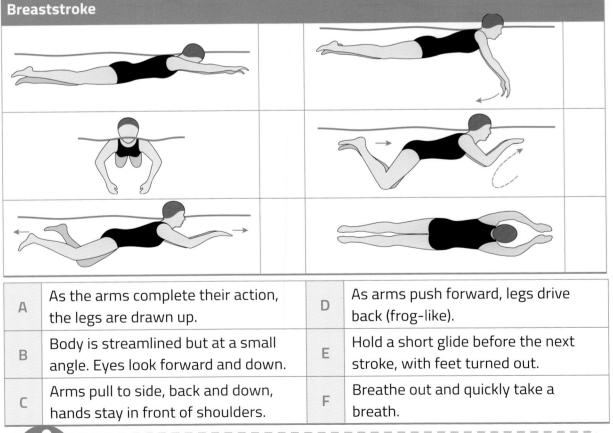

A	As the arms complete their action, the legs are drawn up.	D	As arms push forward, legs drive back (frog-like).
B	Body is streamlined but at a small angle. Eyes look forward and down.	E	Hold a short glide before the next stroke, with feet turned out.
C	Arms pull to side, back and down, hands stay in front of shoulders.	F	Breathe out and quickly take a breath.

 The breaststroke is the slowest Olympic swimming stroke, but it is also the oldest known stroke.

Analyse your technique

LO 3.6 Take responsibility for improving my own performance, based on personal strengths and developmental needs.

Your partner will observe your stroke technique at the beginning and end of the lesson(s). Following the first observation, take their feedback and begin to work on the elements that would improve your technique. Choose a swimming stroke and set yourself a SMART goal.

My SMART Swimming Goal:

Feedback form

Observer name: _____   Review date: _____

Stroke: _____

One strong point:

One thing to work on:

Feedback form

Observer name: _____   Review date: _____

Stroke: _____

One strong point:

One thing to work on:

Aquafit

Water provides resistance, which makes your muscles work harder; and buoyancy, which reduces impact on your joints. This means that you can do activities that raise your heart rate to the training zone with the added fun and novelty of working out in water, and all while helping to build water confidence.

For every action there is an equal and opposite reaction.
(This is Newton's Third Law.)

Have you ever tried aqua zumba, aqua kickboxing, aqua aerobics or aqua HIIT (high-intensity interval training)? Search for them online and see if any of them would interest you.

Here are a few exercises you can do in water to develop your cardiovascular endurance and help meet your MVPA target. See page 220 for a link to some more exercises.

→ **Pool walk (forwards and backwards):** Use a breaststroke arm action as you walk.

→ **Lunge:** Lengthen your stride to lunge to a comfortable depth.

→ **Cross-country ski:** Move opposite leg and arm in sync.

→ **Pool jog**

→ **Knee lifts:** Use the same knee/alternating knees/cross right knee towards left elbow.

→ **Twist:** Stand in one spot, twisting your hips.

→ **Tuck jumps**

→ **Cardio bounce:** Feet apart, soft knees, spring forwards as far as possible. Bounce on the spot once and repeat spring action immediately. Use arms to propel you forwards by cupping hands and sweeping close to the body.

In groups of three or four, design a 10-minute aquafit session. Put together a sequence of exercises which you will lead the class in. Provide clear and simple instructions – it can be difficult to hear in the pool. If you are permitted to play music, choose music that has a strong, clear beat. Check if you have raised the group members' heart rates to the target training zone.

Aquafit Plan of Action

Group members	
Class	
Date	
Fitness component	

Movement skills used	Walking ☐ Jogging ☐ Tuck jumps – forward ☐ Tuck jumps – backward ☐ Pendulum ☐	Dodging side to side ☐ Cardio bounce ☐ Kicking ☐ Sculling ☐ Lunges ☐	Cross-country ski ☐ Twists ☐ Knee lifts ☐ Other: _____ ☐ _____ ☐

Order/sequence of exercises	
Duration	

Number of students per station: _____

Pool area/location of stations/ formation	
Music	

Now review your experience.

What worked well?

_____

_____

What would have made the session better?

What did you learn about effective communication?

What advice would you give to another group about delivering this session?

If the session is not demanding enough you will need to look at the 'overload' principle of fitness.

How would you adapt the session using the overload principle? Think FITT!

1

2

3

4

Water Safety

LO 3.5 Respond appropriately to a range of water safety scenarios.

Recognising water hazards

With a partner, put these hazards in the place where you are most likely to find them: swimming pool; sea and coastal areas; or inland water sites. Add the letter to the row below.

A	Speed of the water	H	Cold water
B	Sudden depth changes	I	Debris and pollution
C	Hidden hazards – weeds, rocks, debris	J	Other swimmers
D	Waves and tides	K	Steps/hoists
E	Different depths	L	Slippery surfaces
F	Trip hazards	M	Offshore winds
G	Canal locks and weirs	N	Dangerous banks

Swimming pool	
Sea and coastal areas	
Inland water sites	

Staying safe around water

Let's consider some personal rules and skills in staying safe around water.

Stop and think:

→ Water is always moving.

→ The water is colder than you think.

→ Edges can be dangerous.

→ There may be dangers under water.

Stay together:

→ Never swim alone – stay close to a friend or family member.

→ Find a safe place to go – only swim in the sea where there is a lifeguard.

→ Plan your activity – check the weather, tide times, get local advice and wear the right clothing for your activity.

Float:

→ If you fall in, float until you feel calm.

→ Signal for help – raise one hand in the air and shout for help.

→ If you can, swim to safety or hold on to something that floats.

→ Keep warm if you can't swim to safety, using the heat escape lessening position (HELP) or huddle position (see p. 237).

Call 999 or 112:

→ If you see someone in trouble in the water, call 999 or 112.

→ Never enter the water to save others.

→ Look for something you can throw to help them float like a life ring or even a football.

→ Keep watch until help arrives.

Survival in water
Treading water

> **When someone is treading water, how do you know that they are doing it successfully?**
>
> **1** _____
>
> **2** _____
>
> **3** _____

You can use one of four different kicks for treading water.

Try each method and put them in order from 1 (most effective) to 4 (least effective) for you.

Breaststroke	Leg action from breaststroke kicking downwards	
Cycle	Similar leg action to cycling a bicycle	
Egg beater	Exert a continuous downward pressure. Knees wider than hips and at 90 degrees to trunk. Knees stay at this level and kick alternately in a cycling movement.	
Flutter	Front crawl leg kick while body is more or less vertical	

Huddle and HELP positions

1 If a group of people are together in the water they can huddle together to conserve body heat, support each other and provide a larger target for rescuers.

2 HELP position (heat escape lessening position):

→ Keep arms tucked close to chest.

→ Keep legs together pointing diagonally down into the water.

What are the benefits of the HELP and huddle positions in water survival?

HELP: _____

_____

Huddle: _____

Land-based rescues
Talk and rescue

→ Raise the alarm.

    ● Dial 999 or 112. You will be asked to give your location and explain what has happened.

    ● Shout and signal to attract others to help and let the person in the water know they have been seen.

→ Try throwing something that floats that they can hold on to while they wait for help.

→ Give clear instructions, e.g. 'Kick your legs'; 'Swim towards me.'

→ Use hand signals and a loud voice to help guide the person to safety.

→ Keep watching and calling to encourage them to swim to safety.

→ If you can, use a long stick, a scarf or anything else you can find to reach the person. Crouch or lie down so that you are not pulled in.

How would you ensure your own safety and stability so that you do not get pulled into danger when helping someone:

From the bank? _____

_____

Standing in shallow water? _____

_____

Self-assessment

Complete the following self-assessment as honestly as possible.

> LO 3.4 Perform competently and confidently in a range of swimming strokes.

I have demonstrated this by my ability to:		
Enter and leave the pool safely	Looking at it	☐
	Working on it	☐
	Nailed it	☐
Regain balance and float	Looking at it	☐
	Working on it	☐
	Nailed it	☐
Swim an agreed distance in a selected swimming stroke	Looking at it	☐
	Working on it	☐
	Nailed it	☐
Swim an agreed distance in a second swimming stroke	Looking at it	☐
	Working on it	☐
	Nailed it	☐
Actively participate in lesson activities	Looking at it	☐
	Working on it	☐
	Nailed it	☐

LO 3.5 Respond appropriately to a range of water safety scenarios.

I have demonstrated this by my ability to:		
Identify the different forms of water risk	Looking at it	☐
	Working on it	☐
	Nailed it	☐
Understand my role as a first responder	Looking at it	☐
	Working on it	☐
	Nailed it	☐
Recognise and evaluate the range of buoyancy aids available	Looking at it	☐
	Working on it	☐
	Nailed it	☐
Communicate clearly with the person in danger and with others	Looking at it	☐
	Working on it	☐
	Nailed it	☐
Select the appropriate rescue response method for the relevant subject	Looking at it	☐
	Working on it	☐
	Nailed it	☐
Successfully perform and evaluate a rescue	Looking at it	☐
	Working on it	☐
	Nailed it	☐

> **LO 3.6** Take responsibility for improving my own performance, based on personal strengths and developmental needs.

I have demonstrated this by my ability to:		
Assess my confidence in water-based activities	Looking at it	☐
	Working on it	☐
	Nailed it	☐
Accurately analyse my performance in a selected stroke	Looking at it	☐
	Working on it	☐
	Nailed it	☐
Set a SMART goal	Looking at it	☐
	Working on it	☐
	Nailed it	☐
Use various drills to improve my technique	Looking at it	☐
	Working on it	☐
	Nailed it	☐
Listen actively and ask questions to help my learning	Looking at it	☐
	Working on it	☐
	Nailed it	☐
Make responsible decisions when working towards goals	Looking at it	☐
	Working on it	☐
	Nailed it	☐
Review and evaluate my progress	Looking at it	☐
	Working on it	☐
	Nailed it	☐

Reflecting on my learning

One thing I am most proud of:

_____

One thing that really helped me to learn:

_____

I really enjoyed:

_____

because _____

The Aquatics CBA

Aquatics seeks to develop in the student:

→ confidence in the water

→ competence in, and an understanding of, basic water safety and life-saving skills and an ability to make decisions having assessed hazards which relate to water activities

→ an awareness of the value of aquatics as a fitness-promoting activity.

Performance assessment in Aquatics

Students are assessed on their ability to respond effectively and safely to a water safety scenario including, where appropriate, entry into water and survival swimming.

There are three aspects to the assessment of a water safety scenario:

→ Appropriate response to a water safety scenario

→ Adherence to the rules of water safety

→ An ability to reflect on their overall learning in the strand.

In this assessment, students are required to demonstrate their ability to respond safely and effectively to a water safety scenario. It is important that every student, irrespective of their competence in swimming, should be able to complete this assessment. In this context, it may be necessary to design more than one water safety scenario requiring a different response depending on the level of swimming competence that the student has. The scenario should be appropriately demanding for the student, depending on their competence in swimming.

On completing their performance assessment in *Aquatics*, students are required to reflect on their overall learning in this strand.

Sample water safety scenarios

Sample water safety scenario 1

You have just started swimming lessons in your local pool. You are making progress but cannot yet swim a width or swim out of your depth. On a day out with your family, you see a young child in distress in shallow water at the beach. Demonstrate what action you would take.

Sample water safety scenario 2

You are have just started swimming lessons in your local pool. You are making progress but cannot yet swim a width or swim out of your depth. A young child falls in at a pier. Demonstrate what action you would take.

Sample water safety scenario 3

You have been learning to swim now for some years and can swim a number of lengths and out of your depth. You are at the beach with some friends. One of them swims out after a ball and gets into difficulty. She is swimming back to shore and is nearly within her depth but visibly tired. Demonstrate what action you would take.

Sample water safety scenario 4

You are on the school swimming team and have been swimming with your club from an early age. You are out boating with your family and you are all wearing buoyancy aids. Three of you are playing on deck and suddenly find yourselves in the water. Demonstrate what action you would take.

Assessment features of quality

Exceptional:

→ The performance demonstrates an excellent response to a water safety scenario.

→ The performance displays an excellent understanding of the rules of water safety.

→ The student's reflection is of excellent quality.

Above expectations:

→ The performance demonstrates a very effective response to a water safety scenario.

→ The performance displays a very good understanding of the rules of water safety.

→ The student's reflection is of very good quality.

In line with expectations:

→ The performance demonstrates an effective response to a water safety scenario.

→ The performance displays a good understanding of the rules of water safety.

→ The student's reflection is of reasonable quality.

Yet to meet expectations:

→ The performance demonstrates an unsatisfactory response to a water safety scenario.

→ The performance displays a basic understanding of the rules of water safety.

→ The student's reflection is limited.

CBA Reflection Form – Aquatics

Consider using some of these words in your reflection:

Word Bank			
buoyancy aid	hypothermia	balance/overbalance	scenario
wade	calm	measured	assured
communicated	controlled	depth	clarity
ability	condition	stable	secure

1 **What were the key facts you noted in the scenario?**

2 **How did you communicate with the person in danger?**

3 **How did you remain safe and calm yourself?**

4 What steps did you take in undertaking the rescue?

5 When did you know that the rescue was completed safely?

6 Is there anything you would have done differently?

Reflection Review Checklist

● I named the water-based scenario I dealt with.	
● I identified the range of options available to me.	
● I explained my choice of rescue.	
● I describe how I undertook the rescue.	
● I evaluated how effective my rescue was.	
● I outlined how I might improve my performance.	
● I used 5–10 of the word bank terms.	

Signature:

Date:

Orienteering and Team Challenges

Looking at it ☐   Working on it ☐   Nailed it ☐

This part of your course helps you to prepare for safe and confident participation in adventure-type activities – such as orienteering – that generally take place in the great outdoors. You will be introduced to basic navigation skills, which will help you to find your way using a map and sometimes a compass. This is a skill that will help you to become an independent traveller anywhere in the world, from Bali to Ballyhaunis!

Orienteering is a competitive sport undertaken individually or in relay teams. Participants follow a course drawn on a map, taking the orienteering controls in order and completing the course as fast as possible. The challenge is between you, the course and the terrain. The winning participant will make clever route choices and use orienteering strategies to successfully collect the orienteering controls. The fastest runner will not always be the winner. This is why the sport is often called 'cunning running'.

Adventure activities will also involve working in teams and making decisions in response to team challenges in a way that helps the team to get stronger and be successful.

 Orienteering is a sport that began in Scandinavian countries at the turn of the 20th century, with training exercises set for the military in the mountains and forests. You can now compete in orienteering events designed specifically for foot, mountain bike, skis and wheelchair.

 I wonder How are the members of a team like pieces of a jigsaw?

My thoughts: _____

_____

At the end of this unit I will be able to:

Learning Outcomes Strand 3: Orienteering and Team Challenges	Year 1	Year 2	Year 3
3.1 Use orienteering strategies and map-reading skills to compete in a variety of orienteering events safely and confidently, showing respect for the environment			
3.2 Contribute to team challenges that require co-operation and problem-solving skills to achieve a common goal			
3.3 Reflect on my personal contribution and my team's effectiveness in completing a group challenge			

Class Challenge:

_____

_____

_____

My Personal Challenge:

_____

_____

_____

Irish Orienteering Association resources: www.orienteering.ie/video-3

New to orienteering? www.basoc.org.uk/info/ new-to-orienteering

Orienteering

Orienteering terminology

Control	A checkpoint on a pre-planned orienteering route, usually marked by a red and white flag.
Map legend	A legend on a map is a description of all the symbols and colours used on the map.
Setting	Orienting (turning) the map so that it lines up exactly with the features on the ground.
Thumbing	Keeping your thumb at the point where you are on the map as you move along the route.
Attack point	Any feature close to the target control site that is obvious and easy to find and can be run towards at pace.
Handrails	Any line feature such as a stream, fence, wall or path that can be followed (held on to) to help you get from one control site to the next.
Check-off features	When moving from one point on a course to the next, some features, e.g. path junctions, buildings, obvious bends on the track, can be identified. When you arrive at these points you can check them off, confirming that you are securely en route.
Catching features	Significant features in the terrain that lie beyond the control site, indicating that you have overshot the target.
Leg	A section of an orienteering course between two consecutive control sites, e.g. control no. 2–3 is a leg of the course.
SI card	An electronic device worn by the orienteer to register arriving at a control. The device is inserted into a battery-operated encoder unit at each control site. The encoders provide a complete progress record of the runner. The final results are downloadable to a computer at the finish.

What makes a successful orienteer?

Look at the attributes surrounding the orienteer. Select the five most important characteristics that would help to make a successful orienteer. Be able to explain your selection.

1	
2	
3	
4	
5	

What attributes do you have that would make you a good orienteer?

1	
2	
3	
4	
5	

Components of fitness for an orienteer

Competitive orienteers require a particular type of fitness in order to perform successfully. The main fitness components are outlined below.

Read each description carefully and select the component in the diagram which it best describes. Put the description number in the box beside the appropriate component.

Capacity to move fluently when running	
Capacity to run hard for short bursts uphill or over difficult terrain	
Capacity to run fast; downhill or in a sprint	
Capacity to maintain a good running speed without becoming tired	
Capacity to run strongly uphill or over difficult terrain	
Capacity for the muscles to continue working throughout the event	

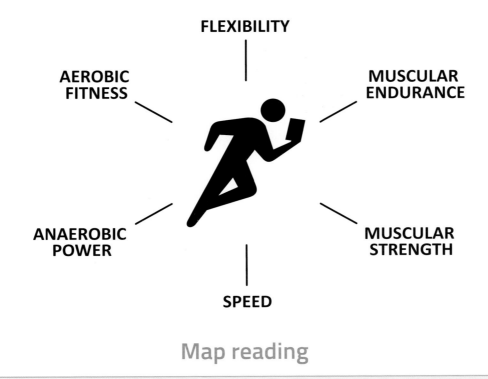

Map reading

> **LO 3.1** Use orienteering strategies and map-reading skills to compete in a variety of orienteering events safely and confidently, showing respect for the environment.

Recognising the symbols and colours

The symbols used on orienteering maps are the same everywhere in the world. The map legend shows the symbols and colours used on the map.

Reading the map: Go to www.orienteering.ie, click on 'What is Orienteering?' and scroll down to 'Video Resources'. Then click on 'Reading the Map 1'.

Legend master

Study the legend on the map below. Now cover the legend with a piece of paper and see how many of the following features you can identify and draw. Check back to the legend to see how many you got right.

High fence	Dirt path/track
Single tree	Building
Area of dense vegetation	Crag
Marshy ground	Boulder

Draw your map

Using the correct symbols and colours, draw an orienteering map of the landscape shown below. Be careful with the shape of features and with the scale (the size of items in relation to each other). Use a pencil and a ruler and have an eraser handy in case you need to re-draw. Do not write names of features on the map.

My Map

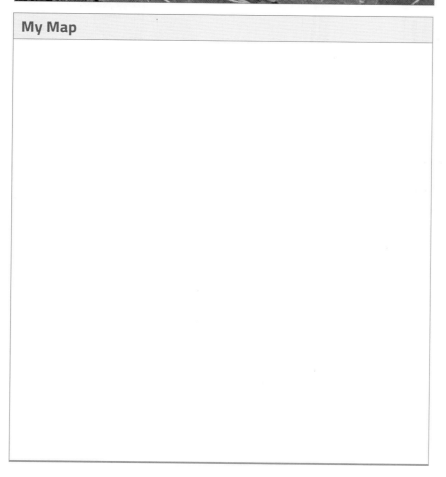

Setting the map

An orienteering map is a simplified and reduced version of the real landscape. There is only one correct way to hold the map so that it matches the features on the ground. The map could be upside down and still be 'set' correctly. Setting the map makes it easier to work out which direction you need to go.

In the following series of maps, only one map is correctly set with each landscape image at the top. Circle the letter where the map fits the terrain picture correctly. Note the shape of features in the picture first and then work back to the map.

Orientating the map: Go to www.orienteering. ie, click on 'What is Orienteering?' and scroll down to 'Video Resources'. Then click on 'Orientating the Map'.

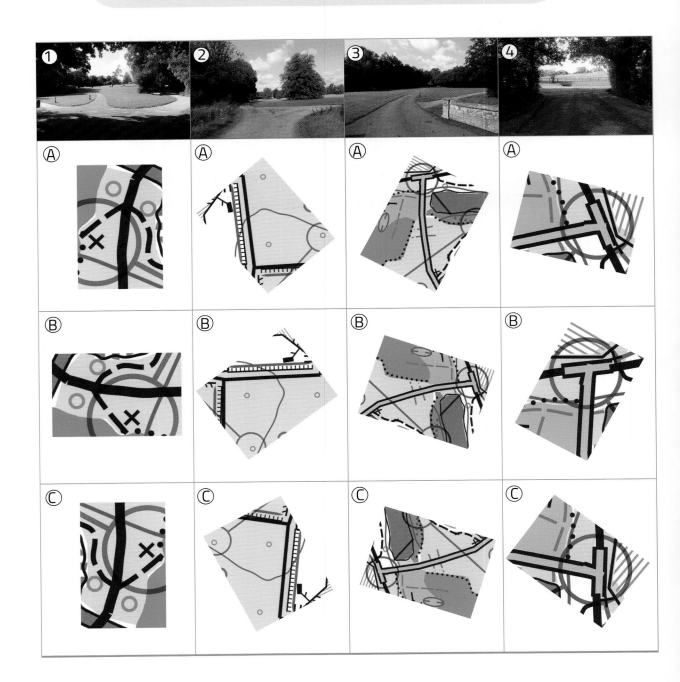

Thumbing the map

Your thumb is your best friend when you are making your way around an orienteering course. Place your thumb beside your current position on the map. The next time you stop, reposition your thumb. Fold the map so that you can hold it securely and reach your location on the map with your thumb. It is really important to keep connected to the map.

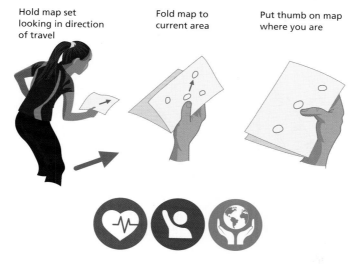

Hold map set looking in direction of travel

Fold map to current area

Put thumb on map where you are

With your partner, follow a route provided by your teacher. Review your use of these navigation skills as you followed each route.

Skills	Forgot	Sometimes	All the time
Thumbing the map			
Setting the map			
Following the route			

Orienteering strategies

Orienteering strategies help you to navigate from one control point to the next. These strategies were explained earlier. Can you remember what they are?

Write a description of each strategy in your own words.

Orienteering strategy	Description
Handrails	
Check-off features	
Catching features	
Attack point	

Look at the map section below. Imagine that you are travelling from control no. 5 to control no. 6. Can you identify features you would select as a handrail, check-off feature, catching feature and attack point? Estimate the distance between control no. 5 and control no. 6. Afterwards, continue to look at other legs of the course.

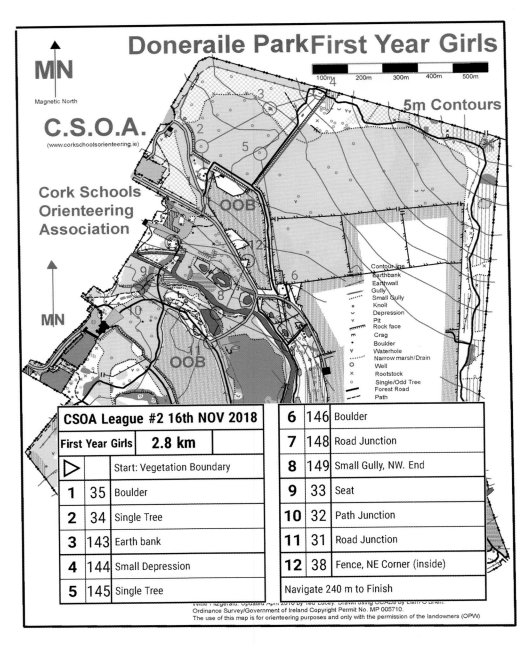

Doneraile Park **First Year Girls**

MN — Magnetic North

C.S.O.A.

(www.corkschoolsorienteering.ie)

Cork Schools Orienteering Association

5m Contours

MN

Legend:
- Contour line
- Earthbank
- Earthwall
- Gully
- Small Gully
- Knoll
- Depression
- Pit
- Rock face
- Crag
- Boulder
- Waterhole
- Narrow marsh/Drain
- Well
- Rootstock
- Single/Odd Tree
- Forest Road
- Path

CSOA League #2 16th NOV 2018		
First Year Girls	**2.8 km**	
▷		Start: Vegetation Boundary
1	35	Boulder
2	34	Single Tree
3	143	Earth bank
4	144	Small Depression
5	145	Single Tree

6	146	Boulder
7	148	Road Junction
8	149	Small Gully, NW. End
9	33	Seat
10	32	Path Junction
11	31	Road Junction
12	38	Fence, NE Corner (inside)
Navigate 240 m to Finish		

Handrail	
Check-off feature	
Catching feature	
Attack point	
Distance from control no. 5 to control no. 6	

Know the Country Code

> **LO 3.1** Use orienteering strategies and map-reading skills to compete in a variety of orienteering events safely and confidently, showing respect for the environment.

We are all responsible for taking care of our environment. It is a precious and fragile resource. A mountaineer's motto is 'Only take photographs and only leave footprints.' When in the countryside you have an obligation to leave it as you found it – or better than you found it!

Here are some ways of protecting our environment. Can you think why each rule is part of the Country Code?

Country Code	Why should I?
Fasten all gates	
Take your litter home	
Help keep water sources clean	
Keep dogs under control	
Do not make unnecessary noise	
Guard against all risks of fire	
Keep to public paths across farmland	
Use gates and stiles to cross fences, hedges and walls	
Protect wildlife, plants and trees	
Leave livestock, crops and machinery alone	

Going to an orienteering event

LO 3.1 Use orienteering strategies and map-reading skills to compete in a variety of orienteering events safely and confidently, showing respect for the environment.

Here are a few key things to remember when you attend an orienteering event. It is important to be aware of the procedures and normal safety expectations that are in place.

Event protocol:

→ Register for the event.

→ Select the appropriate course for your age, class and ability.

→ Check out-of-bounds areas and map corrections.

→ Go to the starting point in good time.

→ Compete on your own or participate with a partner.

→ Take controls in the correct order.

→ Report to the finish.

In the spirit of the event:

→ Make space for other participants.

→ Leave controls as you found them.

→ Comply with out-of-bounds areas.

→ Respect the Country Code.

Safety:

→ Wear a watch.

→ Carry a whistle : six short blasts followed by one long one means HELP.

→ Wear full body cover (no shorts).

→ Choose light footwear with a good grip.

→ Select the appropriate course level (be realistic – check the distance).

→ Have an escape route strategy/a cut-off time.

→ Pace yourself.

→ **ALWAYS** report to the finish.

Team Challenges

> **LO 3.2** Contribute to team challenges that require co-operation and problem-solving skills to achieve a common goal.

Team challenges are a great way to build teamwork and resilience. Each team combines the strengths of its members to overcome various challenges. Good communication and working with others are key skills here. An effective team will look after the welfare of all its members. The outcome depends on each team member's attitude, focus and commitment.

What is a challenge?

Why should you challenge yourself in life?

In a group, discuss what attributes a successful team demonstrates. Add your thoughts to the segments of the wheel below. One has been added to get you started.

Committed to a common goal

'I will pay more for the ability to deal with people than any other ability under the sun.'

John D. Rockefeller

When we work together we should think GROUPS.

Look at the things that help you to work successfully as a group and say why they might help.

Why should I?	
Give encouragement	
Respect others	
On task (stay)	
Use a quiet voice	
Participate actively	
Stay in the team	

Problem-solving approach

Having an organised way of approaching a problem – a plan – increases your chances of being successful in dealing with it. Here are some steps to practise when undertaking team challenges in class.

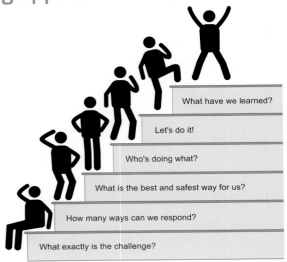

What have we learned?

Let's do it!

Who's doing what?

What is the best and safest way for us?

How many ways can we respond?

What exactly is the challenge?

During your participation in the following challenges you might catch yourself having some negative thoughts. If you do, see if you can change the thoughts on the left to the ones on the right. Try to imagine a better way of approaching challenges you encounter.

Instead of ...	Try thinking ...
I'm no good at this	What am I missing?
I give up	I'll use a different strategy
It's good enough	Is this really my best work?
I can't make this any better	I can always improve
This is too hard	This may take some time
I made a mistake	Mistakes help me to learn
I just can't do this	I'm going to train my brain
I'll never be that smart	I will learn how to do this
Plan A didn't work	There's always Plan B
My friend can do it	I'll learn from them

Try these team challenges. Consider the Key Skills and Wellbeing Indicators for each challenge. After each challenge, think about any advice you might share with other groups.

Challenge 1: Ball toss

Materials: 5 balls per group (size dependent on skill level).

Instructions: A group of 8 students form a circle approximately 5 metres in diametre. The group leader begins with 5 balls. The first ball thrown will begin the sequence that will be repeated each time. The ball may not be passed to a player either side of the thrower. Each player can only receive the ball once. The final throw is back to the group leader.

Once the sequence is established, the group leader adds another ball until all five balls are in play. The group will be successful when all five balls have been in play and returned one by one to the group leader.

Begin again if:

→ a ball falls to the ground

→ a player ends up with a second ball in hand.

Reflection

We demonstrated these Key Skills (see p. viii):

when we:

We demonstrated these Wellbeing Indicators (see p. ix):

when we:

A key piece of advice I would give is:

Challenge 2: Turning over a new leaf

Materials: 4 sheets of heavy-duty plastic or tarpaulin, 2 sheets measuring 1.5 m x 1.5 m; 2 sheets measuring 1.5 m x 1 m.

Instructions: Get into two groups of six. All six members of each group stand on a sheet or tarpaulin. The aim is to get everyone standing on the other side of the sheet without anyone stepping off it. The smaller the surface area the more creative the group has to become to make sure that everyone remains on the sheet and not touching the floor.

Begin again if: a team member steps off the sheet on to the floor.

Variation: Change to the smaller sheet and note the difference.

Reflection

We demonstrated these Key Skills (see p. viii):

when we: _____

We demonstrated these Wellbeing Indicators (see p. ix):

when we: _____

If you turned over both sheets – the larger and the smaller – which challenge did you learn most from? Why?

Challenge 3: Pulling the cord

Materials:

→ 1 perforated piece of Wavin pipe per team
→ 1 piece of cord per team member
→ 3 tennis balls per team
→ 4 cones – target markers A (x2) and B (x2)
→ 1 container per team

Instructions: Place the cones (A and B) 10 metres apart and place the containers at point B. Move the tennis balls, one at a time, from point A to point B. The items may only be moved using the pipe and cords. All team members must be involved. At point B finer degrees of control will be required to drop the ball into the container.

261

Begin again if:

→ a ball falls to the ground

→ not all team members are holding a cord

→ the item does not fall into the container

→ a team member is holding the cord within arm's length of the pipe.

Reflection

We demonstrated these Key Skills (see p. viii):

when we:

We demonstrated these Wellbeing Indicators (see p. ix):

when we:

A key piece of advice I would give is:

Team challenge reflection

> **LO 3.3** Reflect on personal contribution and team effectiveness in completing a group challenge.

Assess your overall performance as a team. Your attitude is like WiFi – it transmits a signal. If you are strong as a team, you will select four bars; if you are very weak, you will select one bar. Shade each signal as appropriate.

Our first reaction was:	4	Bring it on – we can do this	
	3	Let's be positive	
	2	Not sure we can do this	
	1	We're not bothered	
When difficulties were encountered	4	We took it in our stride	
	3	We stayed positive	
	2	We were confused	
	1	We blamed each other or opted out	
On completion we felt	4	We did well	
	3	We did our best	
	2	We could have done better	
	1	We were glad it was over	

Overall Teamwork Assessment	
What are we good at?	
What do we need to work at?	
One change that would make a difference to our teamwork.	

I wonder When you encounter difficulties, what will help you to build resilience or 'grit'?

My thoughts:

Self-assessment: Working with Others

	Never	Sometimes	Always
I listen carefully to other team members.			
I give my opinion without fear of put-downs.			
I make allowances for others.			
I play a full and active part.			
I speak respectfully.			
I trust my team will take care of me.			
I stay focused.			
I can let go and move on.			

Which is your strongest Wellbeing attribute?	
Which attribute do you need to work on?	
Where else in real life is this attribute needed?	
What steps can you take to build that attribute?	

Self-assessment: Orienteering

Make an honest assessment of your orienteering skills and strategies by choosing one of the following in response to each statement: Never/Sometimes/Always.

	Never	Sometimes	Always
I know the symbols and colours on the map.			
I fold the map to the relevant section.			
I set my map by aligning it to the terrain.			
I stay in contact with the map by moving my thumb.			
I identify key check-off features on the map.			
I identify possible handrails on the map.			
I follow the correct event procedures.			
I know where I am on the map.			
I am sure of the distance I travel.			
I identify features in the landscape on the map.			
I think ahead to the next control while running.			
I investigate possible routes to a control.			
I simplify the route to check-off points.			
I memorise key map details.			
I know when I have made a mistake.			
I stay focused.			
I doubt myself.			
I run out of steam.			

I enjoyed orienteering this much (place a mark between 0% and 100% on the line below).

⟵ ——————————————————————————————— ⟶

0%   100%

The Orienteering and Team Challenges CBA

Students, in groups of three, complete a team orienteering event.

There are four aspects to the assessment of the team orienteering event:

→ The use of map-reading skills and orienteering strategies

→ Adherence to event protocols in orienteering

→ Effectiveness as a team member

→ Ability to reflect on individual performance and their contribution to the team performance.

Students, working in threes, are asked to complete a team orienteering event in the fastest possible time by dividing the controls between them in a manner that maximises the skills and fitness of the group.

Assessment features of quality

Exceptional:

→ The student completes a leg of the team orienteering event very successfully, using an excellent range of orienteering skills.

→ The student demonstrates an excellent understanding of event protocol and safety considerations.

→ The student demonstrates an exceptional ability to work effectively as a member of a team.

→ The student's reflection is of excellent quality.

Above expectations:

→ The student completes their leg of the team orienteering event very successfully, using a wide range of orienteering skills.

→ The student demonstrates a very good understanding of event protocol and safety considerations.

→ The student demonstrates a very good ability to work effectively as a member of a team.

→ The student's reflection is of very good quality.

In line with expectations:

→ The student completes their leg of the team orienteering event successfully, using a variety of orienteering skills.

→ The student demonstrates a good understanding of event protocol and safety considerations.

→ The student demonstrates a good ability to work effectively as a member of a team.

→ The student's reflection is of reasonable quality.

Yet to meet expectations:

→ The student partially completes their leg of the team orienteering event.

→ The student demonstrates a very basic understanding of event protocol and safety considerations.

→ The student's contribution to the team's effort is limited.

→ The student's reflection is limited.

Score event

A large number of controls are distributed around an area and their location and description identified on a map. Each control has a particular points value depending on its difficulty. The challenge is to accumulate the highest number of points in the time allowed (e.g. 30 minutes). Be aware that there is a points penalty for finishing outside the time allowed. This penalty is cumulative: 1 minute over time = 10 points penalty; 2 minutes = 20 points penalty, etc.

I wonder In order to achieve success in orienteering, which of the following is the most important element: map-reading, fitness, problem-solving or teamwork? List them in order of importance.

My thoughts: _____

_____

Thinking through the event

The CBA approaches the score event as a team event. Each team is provided with a brief time period to examine the master map containing the total number of controls. This time provides an opportunity for you to demonstrate effective teamwork and good decision-making. At the conclusion of the planning period, a team will have selected the mix of controls that best suits each member. **Note:** Bunching controls by number, e.g. 1–10, may not be the wisest option.

In your teams you have three minutes to look at this map in detail and consider the following:

→ Which controls fit best together?

→ What is the control difficulty? (The points value is a hint.)

→ What is the physical demand? Uphill/downhill; close by/far away?

→ How many controls could you reasonably get in the time?

→ What selection suits the confidence and competence level of each member?

→ How will you know you are approaching the time limit?

→ Clarify and confirm the plan of action (POA).

→ Check SI card procedure, if using it.

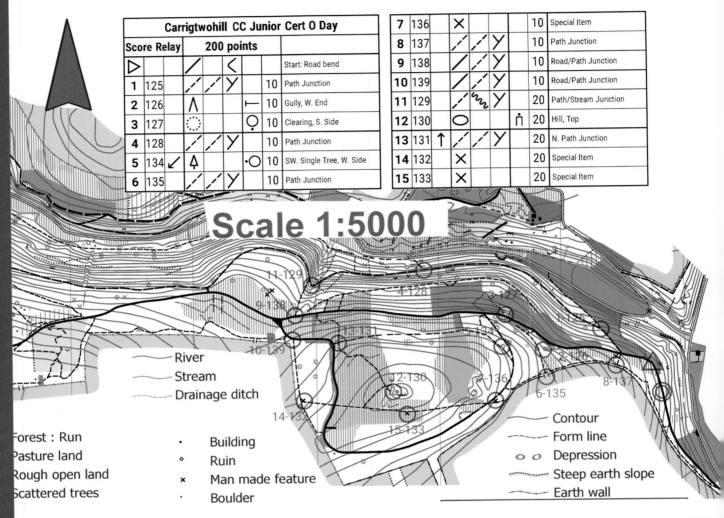

Carrigtwohill CC Junior Cert O Day					
Score Relay		200 points			
▷		/	<		Start: Road bend
1	125		/ Y	10	Path Junction
2	126	∧	⊢	10	Gully, W. End
3	127	○	○	10	Clearing, S. Side
4	128	/ / Y		10	Path Junction
5	134	✓ ⌂	·○	10	SW. Single Tree, W. Side
6	135	/ / Y		10	Path Junction

7	136	×		10	Special Item
8	137	/ / Y		10	Path Junction
9	138	/ / Y		10	Road/Path Junction
10	139	/ / Y		10	Road/Path Junction
11	129	/ 〰 Y		20	Path/Stream Junction
12	130	○	𝝥	20	Hill, Top
13	131	↑ / / Y		20	N. Path Junction
14	132	×		20	Special Item
15	133	×		20	Special Item

Scale 1:5000

River
Stream
Drainage ditch

Forest : Run
Pasture land
Rough open land
Scattered trees

· Building
◦ Ruin
× Man made feature
· Boulder

Contour
Form line
Depression
Steep earth slope
Earth wall

CBA Reflection Form – Orienteering and Team Challenges

Consider using some of these words in your reflection:

Word Bank			
overtime penalty	time limit	points value	control code
strategising	controls	navigate	handrail
calculate	simplify	route choice	working with others
setting	attack point	accumulate	control description
report to finish	collecting features	thumbing	estimated

After the event and when you have the results is the time to reflect on what you have learned from the experience. You will need to think about your individual orienteering performance and your individual contribution to the team.

The hard facts	Controls visited:	
	Points value of my controls:	
	Time taken to complete:	
	Include map and print-out.	
Individual navigation skills	Setting	
	Thumbing	
	Estimating distance	
	Route planning	
Selected leg: Control _____ to _____ Navigation strategies used	Catching features	
	Handrails	
	Attack points	
	Check-off features	
	Running pace	

Individual contribution to the team

1 **I contributed to** team spirit **when I** _____

2 **I contributed my** point of view **when I** _____

3 **I contributed to** clarifying **when I** _____

4 **I contributed to** coping **with difficulties when I** _____

4 I contributed to our **overall result** when I _____

_____

Reflection questions

1 What orienteering skills did I use in completing the event? _____

_____

2 Which skill might I have used better and why? _____

_____

3 One thing that I/we had to work hard at overcoming was _____

_____

and I/we _____

Reflection Review Checklist

● I have included the orienteering map, control card and results print-out (if available).	
● I have identified the controls I was allocated, their points value, the time I took.	
● I described how I complied with event procedures and safety.	
● I have identified the orienteering skills I used.	
● I have given clear examples of orienteering strategies I used from the route I followed.	
● I described how I complied with the Country Code.	
● I outlined how we approached the score event.	
● I explained my contribution to the team.	
● I evaluated how effective our teamwork was.	
● I outlined how we might improve our performance.	

Signature: _____

Date: _____

STRAND 4

Introduction to Dance

Looking at it ☐   Working on it ☐   Nailed it ☐

We use movement as a way of expressing ourselves almost from birth. Dance is a method of connecting with each other and the world around us. Think of the Haka performed by the New Zealand rugby team. This dance strikes fear into the heart of the opposing team, but it is also an expression of Maori culture, representing passion, energy and identity.

Dance not only requires co-ordination, control, balance and physical skill, it also helps develop body awareness. This awareness helps you to be more expressive when performing or choreographing and it helps you understand a performance you are watching.

I wonder What elements make up dance?

My thoughts: _____

_____

At the end of this unit I will be able to:

	Learning Outcomes Strand 4: Dance	Year 1	Year 2	Year 3
4.1	Create a dance on my own or with others, incorporating a selected dance style and a variety of choreographic techniques and suitable props and music			
4.3	Refine my performance based on a critique of a video of my performance and/or feedback from others			
4.4	Perform the dance for an audience incorporating appropriate music and/or props			
4.5	Reflect on my experience of creating and participating in a performance			

Class Challenge:

My Personal Challenge:

Dance terminology

	Definition	Examples
Actions		
Body movements	Using the whole body or part of the body; gestures	Nod, bow, reach, gesture
Types of movement	Using the whole body	Travelling, moving on the spot, turning, falling, balancing, jumping, stretching
Space		
Level	Height from the ground	High, medium, low
Shape	Position of the body	Curved, straight, twisted, angular
Direction	Where you are moving to	Forwards, backwards, diagonally, up, down
Pathways	How you get to where you're going	Curved, straight, zigzag, circular, spiral
Time		
Tempo	The speed of a movement	Fast, medium, slow, accelerating, decelerating
Accent	Putting an emphasis on a certain movement or beat	A sudden or emphasised movement (e.g. a jump) or a sudden stop
Stillness	Holding a position; waiting before moving again	Freeze, pause, delay
Relationships		
Grouping	Formation and size of a group	Solo, duet, ensemble (all together), formations
Interaction	How members of a group interact with each other	Canon, mirroring, partner work
Dynamism		
Energy	Expressing power or tension	Light, heavy, tight, relaxed

Stealthy Ninja

In this activity you're going to become aware of your own personal space, how you and those around you are moving and the type of movements they're making.

Focus: Movement Awareness

You and your partner will each choose two people in the class, Person A and Person B.

You cannot choose the same people. You cannot pick yourselves.

DO NOT tell the people you have chosen!

➡ Stay as far away as possible from Person A.

➡ Stay as close as possible to Person B without them noticing. Ninja style!

Remember, someone is following you too, so make it hard for them!

> **How were you aware of the space around you?**

> **How did your movements change when you were keeping away from Person A and following Person B?**

> **What kind of movements did you make when you were following Person B?**

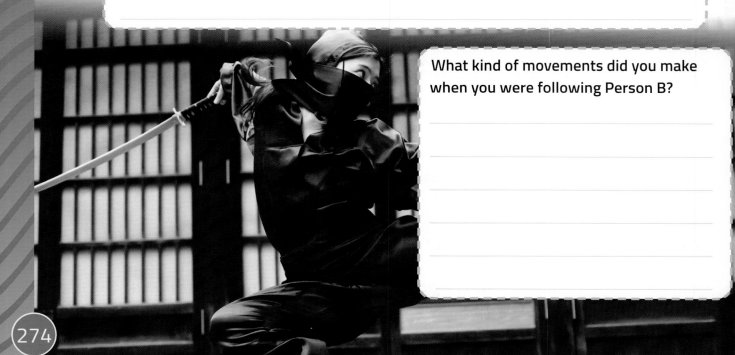

Elements of Dance

Relationships

→ The connection between you and your body, other performers or objects and the shapes created

Time

→ The different ways time affects your movement

Actions

→ The different types of movement you make

Space

→ Your personal, general and performance space and how you interact with it

Dynamism

→ Using strength and power to create different types of movement

Follow me

In this activity you are going to mirror the actions of your partner (duet) to create a sequence of movement.

Focus: Relationships, Actions and Space

Your partner will lead the movement for four counts and then you will swap.

→ **First time:** Standing in one place.

→ **Second time:** Moving in different directions.

→ **Third time:** Moving at different levels and speeds.

→ **Fourth time:** Mirroring – copying the movement of the other person as if in a mirror.

275

How did your movement change from the first time to the third time?

_____

_____

When did you change from moving to dancing? What's the difference?

_____

_____

 I wonder How do flocks of birds fly in complicated formations but never bump into each other?

 Canon: When a movement is repeated by other dancers, each starting at a different time.

Flow: Performing movements smoothly, continuously and confidently.

Go to YouTube and search for 'Dance Toolkit – Choreographic Devices: Canons' (1:30).

Group movement

In a group (ensemble) of four or five, move together around the hall focusing on different elements of dance.

Focus: Actions, Space and Relationships

→ The person at the top of the group controls the movements and the other members copy them.

→ The leader must make four different movements before they face in another direction.

→ When they turn and face in another direction, a new person becomes the leader.

Now see if you can make a flock of your own by joining in with another group.

Where can you see canon in this activity?

What type of grouping is this?

What types of gestures and movements were you making?

How was your flow in this task? How would you improve it?

277

Creating a Dance

LO 4.1 Create a dance on their own or with others.

Pass the move

In your group, each person creates movements for four counts. Everyone in the group copies these movements until it is their turn to lead. Your last movement must tie into the next person's sequence.

When you are performing:

→ Have a clear start and finish.

→ Use different elements of dance.

→ Move with energy and flow.

→ Show confidence by knowing where and when to move, what movement to do and how to do it.

In the boxes below, draw or write the elements you included and how you used them. Use the table on page 273 as a guide.

Which elements did you use?	
Relationships	**Actions**
Grouping	Body movements
Interaction between dancers	Types of movement
Space	
Level	Direction
Shape	Pathway

Action Words

Below are some movements you may have been making so far. These words will help spark some ideas to help you create different dance sequences.

Can you think of any movements not listed? If so, add them to the last column.

	A	B	C	D	E	F	G	H
1	Press	Roll	Turn	Freeze	Punch	Float	Skip	
2	Collapse	Sway	Explode	Rotate	Twirl	Circle	Reach	
3	Leap	Crawl	Twist	Balance	Zig-zag	Skip	Swing	
4	Rise	Creep	Jog	Shiver	Jump	Fall	Quiver	
5	Sway	Bounce	Shake	Slide	Dodge	Bend	Flop	
6	Hang	Drop	Lunge	Sink	Stamp	Melt	Shimmy	

Pick and mix

Pick four words from the table above and see how many different types of movement you and your group can do with them.

Focus: Time, Dynamism

For example, if you choose **rise**, you could rise from the ground, let your arms rise, let your leg rise …

Draw your movements here and describe them.

Action words	Drawing	Description
1 _____		

2 _____		
3 _____		
4 _____		

Poise: Moving gracefully in a balanced way that keeps a clear shape.

Contribution: The part you play in helping your group bring the performance together.

How did each element add to your performance?	
Time	
Tempo	
Accent	
Stillness	
Dynamism	
Energy	

Put your spin on it

Your teacher will give you and your classmates the same four action words from the list on page 279. Each group will have a variation on the same sequence.

Action words	1	2	3	4
My group's variation				
Another group's variation				

What have you learned from this task?

What was the easiest element to include in your sequence? Why?

What was the hardest element to include in your sequence? Why?

Movement map

Create a movement map with your partner using the action words from page 279.

Focus: Tying movements together using the elements of dance.

→ Using the grid on page 279, roll a die to choose which movements to include in your performance. You must pick two movements from each letter group. How many movements is that in total? _____

→ Draw your sequence pattern in the box on page 283.

→ What will the theme of your sequence be? _____.

 Theme: The idea a dance is based on.

Example	Your movement map
Finish	Finish
Rotate	
Run and Reach	
Swing and Melt	
Collapse and Freeze	
Leap	
Roll and Rise	
Crawl	
Zig-zag and Collapse	
Twirl and Jump	
Skip	
Start	Start

LO 4.3 Refine my performance based on a critique of a video of their performance and/or feedback from others.

Feedback

Now watch your classmates' performances and help them make small changes to improve (refine) their performance by giving them feedback. Take note of the different elements of dance you see in their performance.

When they are performing, ask yourself:

→ Is there a clear start and finish?

→ Do they use different elements of dance?

→ Are they moving with poise and energy?

→ Does all this contribute to the performance?

→ Do they show confidence by knowing where and when to move, what movement to do and how to do it?

Elements of dance in the performance:

→ Relationship ☐

One example: _____

→ Actions ☐

One example: _____

→ Dynamism ☐

One example: _____

→ Space ☐

One example: _____

→ Time ☐

One example: _____

Now let's pick out two stars and a wish.

→ **Two stars:** Two things that went well.

→ **A wish:** One thing they could do differently to improve their performance the next time.

Video analysis

Now that you have looked at the different elements of dance, and watched your classmates perform, you're going to figure out what you think makes a good dance. Watch this video and write down what you think makes it a good dance.

> Go to YouTube and search for 'RB DANCE COMPANY | Semi final | France's got talent 2018' (5:22).

I think this is a good dance because:

1	
2	
3	
4	
5	

Now, keeping in mind what you saw, use these criteria to assess the performance:

	Basic	Good	Very Good	Excellent
Skill, poise and confidence				
Delivering the theme				
Creative use of the elements of dance				
Contribution to overall group performance				
Adherence to safety precautions required by the activity				

Styles of Dance

LO 4.1 Create a dance on my own or with others, incorporating a selected dance style.

 I wonder What is the oldest style of dance?

Kahoot quizzes

Hip-Hop Choreography: Go to YouTube and search for 'Dance Toolkit - Hip Hop Choreography' (2:59).

How many different styles of dance can you name?

Street dance
Hip-hop, breakdancing, locking and popping, housedance

Social dance
Cha-cha-cha, waltz, jive, Charleston, quickstep, rock'n'roll, salsa

1970s
Disco

1960s
The twist

1950s
Jive

Classic ballet
Swan Lake

Styles of Dance

The Evolution of Dance

You and your group will create your own 'evolution of dance' routine, showing the evolution of dance using different dance styles.

Focus: Taking responsibility for researching and creating your own routine.

Take three styles of dance from page 287 and develop a routine that connects all three styles.

Do some research and get some inspiration from different sources.

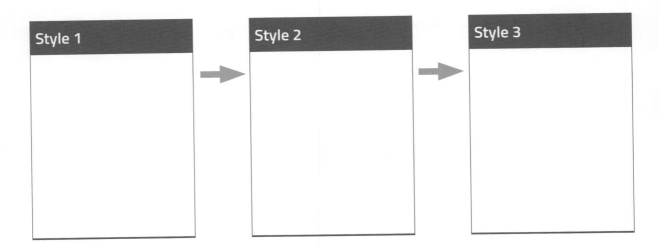

Remember to keep the elements of dance in mind and tick them off as you include them in your map!

Actions		Time	
Body movements		Tempo	
Types of movement		Accent	
Space		Stillness	
Level		Relationships	
Shape		Grouping	
Direction		Interaction between dancers	
Pathway		Dynamism	
		Energy	

Map Your Routine

Mapping out your routine will help you use your space effectively and it will also remind you to include the different elements of dance.

Start

LO 4.3 Refine my performance based on a critique of a video of their performance and/or feedback from others.

Feedback

Now watch your classmates' performances and help them make small changes to improve (refine) their performance by giving them feedback. Take note of the different elements of dance you see in their performance.

When they are performing, ask yourself:

→ Is there a clear start and finish?

→ Do they use different elements of dance?

→ Are they moving with poise and energy?

→ Does all this contribute to the performance?

→ Do they show confidence by knowing where and when to move, what movement to do and how to do it?

Elements of dance in the performance:

→ Relationship ☐

One example: _____

→ Actions ☐

One example: _____

→ Dynamism ☐

→ One example: _____

→ Space ☐

One example: _____

→ Time ☐

One example: _____

Now let's pick out two stars and a wish.

→ **Two stars:** Two things that went well.

→ **A wish:** One thing they could do differently to improve their performance the next time.

LO 4.5 Reflect on my experience of creating and participating in a performance.

Reflection

→ Does your performance show good skill, poise and confidence? How do you know?

→ How did you communicate the style to your audience? Give two examples.

→ Is your performance creative? What new or original ideas did you bring to the routine?

→ How well did you contribute to the overall group performance? How do you know that?

→ What feedback did you get from your classmates?

Choreographic Technique

LO 4.1 Create a dance on my own or with others, incorporating a selected dance style and a variety of choreographic techniques and suitable props and music.

Where to Start?

When someone tells you to be creative, sometimes all the good ideas in your head just fall out! So let's look at some ways to get inspired and create new and interesting movements.

→ **First –** What's your intent (purpose)? What theme/style are you going to use to deliver it?

→ **Second –** Does your music match your intent? Sad music and a happy theme won't go together.

→ **Third –** Look for inspiration from everyday experiences, magazines, YouTube, short video clips or advertisements on TV.

Start by doing some research for new actions!

You Tube

Go to YouTube and search 'How To Come Up With Cool Dance Moves, Concept Choreography | Dance Tips | STEEZY.CO' (3:05).

Here is an example of how you might develop a dance sequence based on Marvel's superheroes.

Sample Dance Sequence

Theme/Style: Superheroes

Intent: To show the different abilities of Marvel's superheroes

Music: *Avengers: Infinity War* Trailer – L'Orchestra Cinematique

0.00	0.47	1.34	2.09	2.33
Start	Slow	Fast	Highlight	Slow	Finish

Inspiration: Images and/or links to videos that helped inspire the dance.

Star-Lord *(Guardians of the Galaxy)*

Go to YouTube and search for 'Star lord dance – Guardians of the galaxy scene | HD 720p' (3:37).

Ceremony Dance *(Black Panther)*

Go to YouTube and search for 'Black Panther Preparing For The Ceremony' (0:54).

Actions:

- **Ironman** – Lunge
- **Vision** – Balance
- **Black Widow** – Crawl
- **Hawkeye** – Rotate
- **Hulk** – Stamp
- **Thor** – Leap
- **Ultron** – Shake
- **Captain America** – Drop

Creating a Dance Sequence

Dancemaker app

This is an example of how choreographic techniques can be used to create a dance sequence.

A → **Core Sequence**
Choose eight movements to use in your first sequence

B → **Retrograde**
Perform the Core Sequence in reverse

C → **Deconstruction**
Take the movements from the Core Sequence and rearrange them

For example:

A → **Core Sequence**
Lunge, Balance, Crawl, Stamp, Rotate, Leap, Shake, Drop

B → **Retrograde**
Drop, Shake, Leap, Rotate, Stamp, Crawl, Balance, Lunge

C → **Deconstruction**
Crawl, Balance, Drop, Lunge, Leap, Rotate, Shake, Stamp

Other techniques you can use to choreograph your routine are:

→ **Repetition:** Repeating a movement sequence in exactly the same way.

→ **Variation:** Varying a sequence that has already been performed by using different dance elements.

→ **Contrast:** Perform parts of the dance in the opposite style, e.g. big/small, fast/slow, high/low.

Repetition and Retrograde: Go to YouTube and search for 'Dance Toolkit - Choreographic Device Repetition and Retrograde' (1:10).

Now that we have chosen the movements, we need to remember to keep the elements of dance in mind!

	Examples
Actions	
Body movements	Lunge, balance, crawl, stamp, rotate, leap, shake, drop
Types of movement	Travelling, moving on the spot, turning, falling, balancing, jumping, stretching
Space	
Level	High, medium, low
Shape	Curved, straight, twisted ...
Direction	Forwards, backwards, diagonally, upwards, downwards
Pathways	Curved, straight, zig-zag, circular, spiral
Time	
Tempo	Fast, medium, slow, accelerating, decelerating
Accent	
Stillness	Freeze, pause, delay
Relationships	
Grouping	Solo, duet, ensemble, formations
Interaction between dancers	Canon, mirroring, partner work
Dynamism	
Energy	Light, heavy, tight, relaxed

Tips for choreographers

1 Why are you doing it? What's your intent?

2 Pick a song. Map out your routine. What are your favourite beats or moments in the song?

3 Use old moves and then add new ones (action words, moves from previous routines).

4 Get inspiration for new moves from everything around you.

5 Take a normal move and switch it up using different dance elements. Maybe alter your body position, change your timing.

6 Practise, practise, practise!

Our Dance Sequence

Our Theme/Style: _____

Our Intent: _____

Music: _____

0.00 _____

Start   Finish

Inspiration: Images and/or links to videos that helped inspire our dance.

Actions:

→ _____

→ _____

→ _____

→ _____

→ _____

→ _____

→ _____

→ _____

→ _____

Designing our sequence

In this activity you will use choreographic techniques and your inspiration from page 292 to create a dance sequence.

Focus: Using Relationships, Actions, Dynamism, Space and Time to vary the movements.

Intent: To perform a dance sequence that clearly shows different choreographic techniques and your chosen theme/style.

| → Core Sequence | → Retrograde | → Deconstruction | → _____ | → _____ |

Remember to keep the elements of dance in mind!

Actions		Time	
Body movements		Tempo	
Types of movement		Accent	
Space		Stillness	
Level		**Relationships**	
Shape		Grouping	
Direction		Interaction between dancers	
Pathway		**Dynamism**	
		Energy	

LO 4.4 Perform the dance for an audience incorporating appropriate music and/or props.

Performance and Self-assessment

Perform your dance for an audience of your choice. Record the performance and, on review, take note of the different elements of dance you see in your performance.

When you are performing, ask yourself:

→ Is there a clear start and finish?

→ Do you use different elements of dance?

→ Are you moving with poise and energy?

→ Does all this contribute to the performance?

→ Do you show confidence by knowing where and when to move, what movement to do and how to do it?

Elements of dance in the performance:

→ Relationship ☐

One example: _____

→ Actions ☐

One example: _____

→ Dynamism ☐

→ One example: _____

→ Space ☐

One example: _____

→ Time ☐

One example: _____

Now let's pick out two stars and a wish.

→ **Two stars:** Two things that went well.

→ **A wish:** One thing they could do differently to improve their performance the next time.

 _____

 _____

 _____

LO 4.5 Reflect on my experience of creating and participating in a performance.

Reflection

→ Does your performance show good skill, poise and confidence? How do you know?

→ Is the style easy to see? How did you make sure it was clear to see?

→ Is your performance creative? What new or original ideas did you bring to the routine? Where did those ideas come from?

➡ How well did you contribute to the overall group performance? How do you know that?

_____

_____

_____

_____

➡ If you could perform this dance routine again, what would you change and why?

_____

_____

_____

The Dance CBA

In the performance assessment for dance or gymnastics, students are required to perform their own dance/gymnastic creation **in a group** of not more than four students. In dance/gymnastics, the student's performance should demonstrate the following:

→ Skill, poise and confidence

→ Understanding of the theme

→ Creative use of choreography and compositional techniques

→ Contribution to overall group performance

→ Adherence to safety precautions required by the activity.

They should also reflect on their experience of creating and participating in a performance.

Assessment features of quality

Exceptional:

→ The performance demonstrates excellent skill, poise and confidence.

→ The performance demonstrates excellently the style/theme on which the final performance is based.

→ There is an excellent level of creativity evident.

→ The student's performance contributes excellently to the overall group performance.

→ The student's reflection is of excellent quality.

Above expectations:

→ The performance demonstrates very good skill, poise and confidence.

→ The performance demonstrates very well the style/theme on which the final performance is based.

→ There is an excellent level of creativity evident.

→ The student's performance contributes very well to the overall group performance.

→ The student's reflection is of very good quality.

In line with expectations:

→ The performance demonstrates good skill, poise and confidence.

→ The performance demonstrates well the style/theme on which the final performance is based.

→ There is a reasonable level of creativity evident.

→ The student's performance contributes well to the overall group performance.

→ The student's reflection is of reasonable quality.

Yet to meet expectations:

→ The performance demonstrates a very basic level of skill, poise and confidence.

→ The performance does not clearly contribute to the style/theme on which the final performance is based.

→ The student's performance makes little contribution to the overall group performance.

→ The student's refection is of limited quality.

CBA Reflection Form – Dance

Consider using some of these words in your reflection:

Word Bank				
relationships	actions	dynamic	space	time
pathways	stillness	accents	energy	repetition
retrograde	deconstruction	elements	confidence	intent
canon	mirroring	flow		

1. I demonstrated the theme/style (supports intent, choice of music, movements, sequences performed) in my sequence when I …

2. I demonstrated energy (e.g. head position, hand action, clear and graceful movement) in my sequence when I …

3. I demonstrated my range of skills (e.g. level of difficulty, balance, solo/duet/ ensemble, jumps) when I …

4. I demonstrated confidence (e.g. timing, start, finish, worked in unison) when I …

5 I demonstrated my creativity (e.g. use of space, time, flow, relationship, choreographic technique, music or prop) when I …

6 My individual contribution to the performance (e.g. lead, follower, choreographer, planner, video analyst, participation, energy) …

7 What was my overall feeling on my performance (e.g. not just a listing or description; I recognise my limitations and strengths)?

Reflection Review Checklist

I named the theme/style on which the sequence is based (e.g. social dance, modern dance).	
I identified points in the sequence where I demonstrate poise (e.g. head position, hand action, extension, graceful movement).	
I identified points in the sequence where I demonstrate confidence (e.g. timing, skill technique, start, finish).	
I identified the range of skills I used (e.g. level of difficulty, inversion, balances, solo/duet/ensemble, jumps).	
I explained how my performance was creative (e.g. use of space, time, flow, relationship, music or props).	
I explained my individual contribution to the performance (e.g. lead, follower, choreographer, planner, video analyst, participation, energy).	
My reflection is an honest judgement of my performance (e.g. not just a listing or description; I recognise my limitations and strengths).	
I have used accurate dance terms in my account.	

Signature: _____

Date: _____

Introduction to Gymnastics

Looking at it ☐   Working on it ☐   Nailed it ☐

Gymnastics provides you with a great opportunity to be creative and to focus on the quality of your movement. Gymnastic movements turn up in lots of places – after goals are scored in soccer matches, in getting around obstacle courses, on the dance floor, in hip-hop moves, in the circus, in parkour and, of course, the floor and apparatus routines in the Olympics.

Gymnastics is concerned with how the body moves. The aesthetic element – the artistic element – is really important, but gymnastics also develops a really sound foundation for the development of competence and confidence in other sports and activities.

 The word 'gymnastics' comes from the Greek word **gymnos**, which means 'nude': most gymnastic training in Ancient Greece took place nude.

 I wonder Are people with big muscles, e.g. body builders, naturally suited to gymnastics because they are so strong?

My thoughts: _____

_____

At the end of this unit I will be able to:

Learning Outcomes Strand 4 (Gymnastics)		Year 1	Year 2	Year 3
4.2	Create a sequence of movement or routine based on a gymnastic theme (on my own or with others), incorporating a variety of compositional techniques and gymnastics skills			
4.3	Refine my performance based on a critique of a video of their performance and/or feedback from others			
4.4	Perform the gymnastics sequence of movement for an audience incorporating appropriate music and/or props			
4.5	Reflect on my experience of creating and participating in a performance			

Class Challenge:

My Personal Challenge:

Go to YouTube and search for '7 Things About... Olympic Artistic Gymnastics' (1:58).

Street-style gymnastics

Gymnastics terminology

Poise	The way you hold yourself – graceful and alert.
Aesthetic	How the movement looks – pleasing to the eye.
Symmetry	One side of the body exactly matches the other.
Asymmetry	One side of the body does not match the other.
Transition	How one movement moves on to the next.
Alignment	The line of the body from top to toe.
Body tension	When muscles tighten to tense the body.
Sequence	A series of movements linked together.
Matching	Two performers exactly match each other's movements.
Mirroring	Two performers reflect (mirror) each other's movements.
Apparatus	Gymnastics equipment, e.g. a gym bench.
Flow	Actions or movements combine smoothly.
Balance	The body is held steady above a base of support.
Inversion	Having your body above the level of your head.
Flight	Actions where the body is airborne.
Technique	A particular way of performing a skill.

Our Gymnastics Rules

What are **your** class rules for gymnastics?

Here are some examples to give you a few ideas.

> ### GYMNASTICS HOUSE RULES
> Keep hands and feet to yourself
> Do only what you are instructed to do
> Wear the correct footwear – no socks
> Keep mats free from obstruction
> No shoes on the mat
> Don't mess about
> No put-downs
> Do your best

With a partner, draw up your own Gymnastics House Rules in the blank circles.

Focus: Being safe in gymnastics class.

307

Safety first!

Footwear

It's best to be barefoot or wear gymnastic socks. Do not wear regular socks as you run the risk of slipping and injury.

Lifting apparatus

Use the correct technique:

→ Lift mats and apparatus with a partner – don't do it on your own.

→ Get close to the object being lifted.

→ Keep a wide, secure base with your feet firmly on the ground.

→ Use your larger leg muscles rather than your back muscles.

→ Tighten your core – abdominal muscles.

→ Keep your back straight when lifting or lowering.

→ Hold the object close to your body.

→ Get assistance if the object is very heavy.

Stop and think   Position the feet   Adopt a good posture   Get a firm grip   Move the feet   Put down then adjust

Control

Challenge yourself progressively – only move to the next level when you have control of your current level.

Warm-up and cool down

The greater your flexibility, mobility and general muscular strength the better. Warming up is important to prepare your body for exercise, help you give your best performance and reduce the risk of injury.

Cool down properly afterwards to bring your body back to a relaxed and recovering state. (Check out warm-up/cool-down in Strand 2, pp. 119–122 for more information.)

What Qualities Make a Successful Gymnast?

Name five characteristics that a successful gymnast needs. Be able to explain your selection.

Focus: What it takes to become a gymnast.

If possible, view a gymnastics performance here:

Go to YouTube and search for 'Gymnastics – Motivational video' (5:45).

1	
2	
3	
4	
5	

 Successful Olympic gymnasts begin their training as early as three years of age.

Consider using some of these words:

confident	risk-taker	flexibility	self-belief	power
agility	co-ordination	balance	muscular endurance	creativity
trust	discipline	control	grace	

Are any of these qualities needed in any other sport/activity? How many can you think of?

Who is this successful Irish gymnast?

_____

 Gymnastics Ireland is the national governing body for gymnastics in Ireland.

Components of Fitness in Gymnastics

To what degree are these components of fitness important for success in artistic gymnastics? Rate each from 1 (= not at all important) to 5 (= extremely important).

Focus: Fitness demands associated with gymnastics.

Success factor	Your rating
Body size and composition	
Aerobic endurance	
Strength and power	
Speed	
Flexibility	
Agility	
Balance and co-ordination	
Reaction time	

Which of these components of fitness would you like to improve during this unit of learning? Try setting yourself a SMART goal.

My SMART goal is:

_____

'Life is not about how fast you run, or how high you climb, but how well you bounce.'

Create a Sequence of Movement

LO 4.2 Create a sequence of movement or routine based on a gymnastic theme.

With a partner, watch and analyse this gymnastics performance.

Go to YouTube and search for 'PE Gymnastics Routine' (2:50).

Consider using some of these words:

quality of movement	poise	control	confidence	creativity
timing	flow	contrast	levels	body shapes
body tension	effort	teamwork		

What qualities must a gymnastics performance demonstrate?

What will it take for you to achieve this level of performance?

Locomotion: Ways of Travelling

Let's look at how we move in gymnastics. Your style of movement is key to gymnastics because how the movement looks, its aesthetic, makes it appealing to the observer – or not!

In how many ways can you travel across the hall?

What makes your travel a gymnastic action?

(a) Attempt each of the following actions. Perform with:

→ muscle tension and extension

→ poise

→ control.

Focus: Moving with style; exploring the quality of movement.

1	Walk forward	8	Walk backwards
2	Spider walk	9	Robot walk
3	Skip	10	Hop on one foot (no more than five times)
4	Jump with both feet	11	Zig-zag run
5	Chassé	12	Step – spin – step
6	Hopscotch	13	Slide
7	Crab walk	14	Scorpion walk

(b) Move through the pattern of your name linking together at least five of these actions.

(c) Add a change of speed: fast pace – slow pace – slow motion.

In what way do changes of direction and changes of speed help the performance?

Change of direction:

_____

Change of speed:

_____

Travel is often used as a link between two more static actions, for example, balance – travel – balance. It is good to develop your range of travelling actions so that you can add variety to your sequence. A sequence is a created by linking a number of gymnastic movements together.

Flight: Jumps

I wonder If you stood on a weighing scales with your hands at your side and swung your arms suddenly and swiftly upwards, what would happen to the needle on the weighing scales? Why?

Jumps have three phases:

→ Take off   → Flight   → Landing

With a partner, try three standing pencil jumps each. Now decide what helps you to:

→ Gain height in your take-off

→ Create a shape

→ 'Stick' the landing.

Focus: Flight control and landing.

Take-off	Flight	Landing

Try these jumps.

1
Pencil jump

2
Star jump

3
Tuck jump

4
Straddle jump

→ First practise the shape while lying on the mat.

→ Put some jumps together in sequence: jump, rebound, jump, rebound, jump, land. Have a clear start and finish.

→ Try a straight jump with a half (180°) and a full (360°) turn.

Focus: Being creative in flight.

Go to YouTube and search for 'GCSE PE Gymnastics Evidence' (3:54).

Using the following criteria, observe your partner and tick when you see what makes a good jump. Feel free to offer advice.

	Pencil	Star	Tuck	Straddle	Notes
Achieved height					
'Stuck' the landing					
Made a clear shape					
Pointed toes					
Executed with poise					

Creativity with Choreography

Changing body shape makes a sequence more interesting. Add a twist!

Take a freeze frame capturing your group's shape in the air. How does it look?

You will need to be able to describe your sequence using pictures. These pictures will act as a really useful aid to help you recall the order of your sequence.

Balances

In gymnastics, a balance is successful when the pose is held for at least three seconds and the body demonstrates tension, extension and poise.

Find a balance that has **four points of contact** with the floor. Move into a different four-point balance.

Find a balance that has **three points of contact** with the floor. Move into a different three-point balance.

Find a balance that has **two points of contact** with the floor. Move into a different two point balance.

Find a balance that has **one point of contact** with the floor. Move into a different one-point balance.

Focus: Feel the muscle tension and look for good extension.

(a) With a partner, select four balances, one from each category on page 315. Put the balances together in a sequence, in any order you like. Use travel as a link between balances. Move smoothly from one balance to the next.

(b) Try the balances in different relationships with your partner: side by side; face to face; one behind the other. Use a mix of matching and mirroring.

Focus: Looking at symmetry and asymmetry to add interest to body shape.

(c) Change the shape: straight, split, straddle, stag and abstract.

(d) Make some balances asymmetrical (A) and some symmetrical (B).

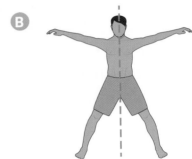

A is an example of non-symmetrical balance. The two sides of the line are *not* the same.

B is an example of symmetrical balance. The two sides of the line *are* the same – if you could fold the person in half at the dotted line, the two sides would match.

You also look at symmetry in your Maths classes. Circle the letters that have reflectional symmetry. Do any letters have more than one line of symmetry?

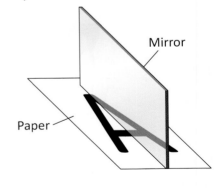

A B C D E F G H I J K L M

N O P Q R S T U V W X Y Z

Matching	Two or more people do exactly the same movement.
Mirroring	Your movement or position is an exact reflection of your partner's.
Unison	You and your partner/s perform movements at the same time.
Canon	You and your partner/s perform your movements one after another – one move prompts/leads into the next.

Use the diagram below to choreograph (design) your sequence. Draw the order of moves in the boxes. Use the links to identify how you will move smoothly between balances.

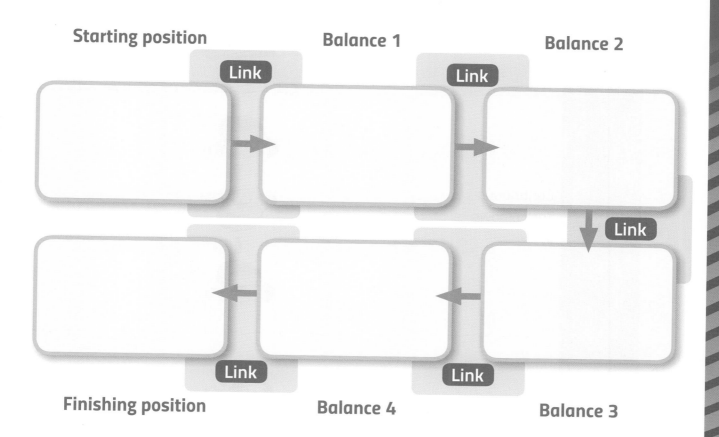

Rotational Movements: Rolls

What do you need to make a roll work?

1 Curved surface area.

Why? _____

2 Transfer (move) your weight.

Why? _____

3 Tight body mass.

Why? _____

Types of roll

How many of the following rolls can you do? See if you can smoothly link together any five of these rolls.

Pencil roll	Flip with hips Arms beside ears	
Egg roll	Continuous Tuck elbows in	
Daisy roll	Closed – open – closed	
Side roll	Sit – reach – roll Elbow push	

Teddy bear roll	Ear to floor Feet wide Elbow push	180°
Forward straddle to pike sit	Chin to chest Hips high Bend elbows Fall over	
Tucked forward roll	'Hedgehog'	
Backward roll to two knees	Chin to chest	
Backward roll to half split	Hands behind head	
Tucked backward roll	Push with arms	

Forward roll – peer assessment

When you have completed the progressions for your forward roll, observe your partner's performance and complete this feedback sheet for them.

Performer: _____

Observer: _____

		Green	Amber	Red
Start with feet together and crouch down				
Reach forward to place hands on mat				
Tuck chin to chest				

⭐
⭐ _____
_____

		Green	Amber	Red
Strong push from **both** feet				
Roll on the shoulders				
Tuck knees to chest				

⭐
⭐ _____
_____

		Green	Amber	Red
Heels to butt				
Reach forward to stand				
Finish tall – arms by ears				

⭐
⭐ _____
_____

Inversion

Inversion is any skill where your body is above your head – for example donkey kick, crane pose, shoulder stand, headstand, handstand, cartwheel, round-off.

Understanding handstands:
Go to YouTube and search for 'Understanding Handstands – The ART Principle' (9:20).

What makes a successful handstand?

In the table below, name the points that will help you to successfully complete a handstand. Work through each phase of the technique.

Focus: Building confidence with weight on hands.

Technique phase	Key points
Lunge	1 _____ 2 _____ 3 _____
Lift and hold	1 _____ 2 _____ 3 _____ 4 _____
Landing	1 _____ 2 _____ 3 _____

Check your criteria with your teacher.

Lunge step   Lift and hold   Landing

Analyse your partner's handstand using the agreed criteria. If you have access to a recording device you can use it to record the handstand.

Cartwheel

Begin here

A cartwheel is a really cool skill – you make your limbs move like the spokes of a turning wheel. Practising your cartwheel will develop your sense of where your body is in space (kinaesthetic awareness). The cartwheel adds energy to a sequence and is the lead-in point to round-off.

What makes a good cartwheel?

View a cartwheel using one of the links below or observing a member of class. Using the criteria you agree with your teacher, identify the technique qualities that are demonstrated.

Focus: Extending and free flow.

www.wikihow.com/ Do-a-Cartwheel

Go to YouTube and search for 'Cartwheel Progressions Sequence Clips' (2:31).

All the power comes from your legs.

→ Reach into the cartwheel.

→ As you place your hands, kick your trailing leg.

→ Your body moves through the vertical – your hips go over the top of your hands.

→ Your arms, hips and legs are aligned.

→ Do not lift your hands off the floor – push the floor away with your hands.

→ Use handprints and footprints to help.

Shoulder Stand

(a) With a partner, experiment with the shoulder stand and see if you can work out a successful technique.

(b) The correct steps in the shoulder stand technique are all mixed up below. Put the following steps in the correct order by writing the correct number in the right-hand column, starting at 1.

Raise hips over shoulders	
Tuck elbows under hips, placing the hands on the lower back for support	
Point toes and tighten core – hold for three seconds	
Curl body up, bringing knees towards your chest	
Extend the legs straight into the air	
Lie flat on your back on the mat	
Move smoothly with control	

(c) In how many ways can you arrive at the shoulder stand?

From lying on back		From lying on stomach	
From sitting		From kneeling	
From standing		Front support	

Gymnastics Sequence Task Card

1 **With a partner or in groups of three, create a sequence that contains:**

→ A clear start and finish

→ Travel actions and balances from the table below

Use your school telephone number, or one your teacher gives you, to choose the actions.

2 **Now add:**

→ Different levels

→ Change of direction

→ Change of speed

3 **Perform your sequence for the class.**

1 Log roll	**2** Leap from one foot to one foot
3 One-foot balance	**4** Jump and land on both feet
5 Side roll	**6** V sit
7 Dish balance (front or back)	**8** Forward roll
9 Two- or three-point balance	**0** Travel using hands

Peer assessment

(a) Identify which criteria you are going to use to judge the performance. Decide what you would expect to see in a good performance. Write each criterion in the grid below.

Criterion	Description	Feedback notes

(b) Having viewed the performance, agree on your judgement and consider what feedback you could offer based on the criteria you have set out.

You nailed it:

The way you _____ was really good because _____

_____ .

The best part of your technique was when you _____ .

Your control was obvious when you _____ .

Work to do:

If you _____ it would help because _____

_____ .

When you _____ , remember to _____

_____ .

Partner Balances
Safety first!

Here are some guidelines to help you be safe, secure and successful when you are working on partner/group balances or building pyramids.

→ **Hand grips:** Interlocked wrists provides a firm and reliable grip when performing counter-tension balances. It helps if your hands are dry.

→ **Lock out joints:** Reduces the pressure on the muscle and provides greater stability.

→ **Use a spotter** in the learning phase. The spotter provides initial support as you gain confidence.

→ **Do not jump** out of or into any partner balance. The risk of falling or injury is multiplied.

→ **Secure the base first:** Close in and lock out for more stability when building upwards.

→ **Soft body parts:** Avoid pressure or weight on fleshy parts of the body such as the belly. Choose hips, knees or shoulders. Do not put pressure on the lower back or spine.

Note: Challenge yourself, but work within the limits of your ability and take it step by step. Sensible and responsible behaviour is important.

Counterbalances

Counterbalance is when two gymnasts depend on each other's weight in order to maintain balance. Working together like this requires trust, co-ordination and awareness of your centre of gravity.

In the counterbalance example provided below, circle where the base of support is for each person and draw a vertical line to identify where the centre of gravity is.

Focus: Working together to locate the point of counterbalance.

 Is the centre of gravity in the same position for men and for women? Have you tried the chair experiment?

What normally happens when your centre of gravity is outside your base of support?

Try these counterbalances with a partner.

Can you locate the centre of gravity in counterbalances A–H?

Partner balances

Using the following criteria, observe another pair perform four counterbalances. Tick the criteria if present in the performance. Offer some feedback based on your judgement. You could record the performance and use still screen grabs to check the criteria.

Paired balances				
Muscle tension				
Extension				
Clear sharp shape				
Held still for three seconds				

1. Perform at least two balances from each line of the image below.

2. Move out of a balance in a different direction, e.g. use twists or rolls.

3. Using rolls, jumps, twists, stepping actions or spins, move into each balance in a controlled way.

4. Select a number of balances and link them together to form a sequence.

5. Record your performance and review the quality of balances, flow (transitions) and change of direction.

6. Teach your sequence to another pair and perform together in unison.

Be creative! Change the shape: straight, split, straddle, stag and abstract.

Focus: Sequence-building and transitions.

Partner balances: Level 1

329

Peer assessment

Observers: _____

_____

Performers: _____

_____

Balances (skill and poise)	I liked the way you _____
	It would be even better if you _____
Transitions (confidence)	I liked the way you _____
	It would be even better if you _____
Change of direction (creativity)	I liked the way you _____
	It would be even better if you _____

What words can you think of to describe the criteria below?

Balance: _____

_____

Transitions: _____

_____

Direction: _____

_____

Group balances

Revisit the safety advice on page 327.

Try the following balances with your group.

→ All balances must demonstrate control and quality.

→ There is scope in each example for your own creativity – change the shape and composition.

→ Discover interesting ways of entering into and exiting each balance.

Focus: Experiment, select, practise, refine and master.

Self-assessment

Complete a self-assessment of your performance. Use the results of your review, or a viewing of a recording, to refine and improve your next performance. In your review, use some of the words from the word bank on page 333.

Based on the feedback I received and having reviewed my performance:

I am happy with:

1 _____

2 _____

3 _____

I need to develop these areas:

My competence in (balance, jumps, etc.): _____

_____

Choreography (space/time/flow): _____

_____

_____

Missing elements (balances, rolls, jumps, etc.):

_____

_____

Poise and confidence:

_____

_____

Signature: _____ Date: _____

I enjoyed the sequence this much:

The best bit was: _____

_____

Consider using some of these words:

shape	aesthetic	levels	direction	pathway
controlled	tension	extension	effort	canon
flow	transitions	synchronised	poise	unison

┌───┐
│ **I learned best when I was able to ...** │
│ │
│ _____ │
│ │
│ _____ │
└───┘

Gymnastics Performance Assessment 1

Perform a paired gymnastics sequence that lasts a minimum of 60 seconds. In your sequence demonstrate quality, control and creativity.

Quality	Poise, muscle tension, alignment, sound technique in a range of skills
Control	Clear start and finish, hold balances for three seconds, timing/synchronisation, landing
Creativity	Different levels, speeds, directions, variety of body shapes, matching/mirroring, unison/canon, use of space, transitions, symmetry/asymmetry

Include the following elements at a minimum:

→ Two different jumps

→ Three different rolls

→ Three individual balances

→ Three paired balances/counterbalances

→ One example of weight on hands (inversion)

→ Three changes in direction.

Reflection

1 What did you enjoy about gymnastics?

_____

2 What did you not enjoy as much about gymnastics?

_____

3 What was your favourite skill to learn?

_____

4 What helped you to learn best in gymnastics?

Gymnastics Performance Assessment 2

In groups of no more than four, perform a gymnastics sequence of 1–2 minutes' duration comprising a series of balances, weight transfer, travelling and transitions. Demonstrate poise, competence and confidence and an awareness of choreographic features. Optional: include apparatus and music.

Planning for your performance

Circle the theme(s) selected:

Balance   Travel   Weight transfer

Choreographic elements:

Using the RADS format, circle the elements included.

Element	Explanation	Examples
Relationships	With whom or what the gymnast is relating as s/he moves	• Individual, partner, group • Supporting, being supported, matching/mirroring, synchronised, unison/canon, to music • Apparatus: in front of/alongside/ behind • Far from/near; meet/part
Actions	What a gymnast does	• Shapes: straight, curved, twisted, symmetry/asymmetry • Flight: jumps, leaps and lifts • Actions: stepping, leaping, roll, balance, stillness, dance-like movements
Dynamics	How the body moves	• Speed: sudden, sustained, fast, slow, pause • Strong/light, transitions, smooth, fluid
Space	Where the body moves	• Forwards, backwards, sideways • Level: high, medium, low • Pathway: varied floor pattern • Planes: sagittal (wheel), frontal (door), horizontal (table)

Include the following balances:

→ Four individual balances – demonstrate your individual skills here

→ Four partner balances

→ Four three-person balances

→ Two quad balances

→ One balance created by the group.

The plan

Draw your selected balances in the boxes. Label group members.

Four individual balances:			
A	B	C	D

Four partner balances:			
E	F	G	H
Group members:			

Four trio balances:			
I	J	K	L
Group members:			

Four quad balances:		Group balance:
M	N	O

Group members:		

Now draw a helicopter view of your pattern of movement on the mat. Use the letters above to map where the balances occur.

Example:

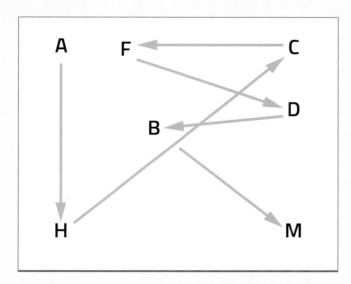

Your plan:

LO 4.3 Refine their performance based on a critique of a video of their performance and/or feedback from others.

Review and refine

Using the following criteria, award your performance a star rating and identify any elements that need attention.

Overall impact	
Poise and confidence	☆ ☆ ☆ ☆ ☆
Work still to do	
Relationships: with whom/what (e.g. in sync with each other, canon/ unison, etc.)	
Actions: what the body does Balance quality Shapes, flight, stability	
Dynamics: how the body moves Flow and timing Are there delays? Changes in speed, smooth transitions	
Use of space: where the body moves Changes of direction Level, pathway	
Team name: _____ Date: _____	

The Gymnastics CBA

In the performance assessment for dance or gymnastics, students are required to perform their own dance/gymnastic creation **in a group** of not more than four students. In dance/gymnastics, the student's performance should demonstrate the following:

→ Skill, poise and confidence

→ Understanding of the theme

→ Creative use of choreography and compositional techniques

→ Contribution to overall group performance

→ Adherence to safety precautions required by the activity

→ Create, refine, perform and review (a sequence of movement) in gymnastics as part of a group of not more than four students.

Assessment features of quality

Exceptional:

→ The performance demonstrates excellent skill, poise and confidence.

→ The performance demonstrates excellently the style/theme on which the final performance is based.

→ There is an excellent level of creativity evident.

→ The student's performance contributes excellently to the overall group performance.

→ The student's reflection is of excellent quality.

Above expectations:

→ The performance demonstrates very good skill, poise and confidence.

→ The performance demonstrates very well the style/theme on which the final performance is based.

→ There is an excellent level of creativity evident.

→ The student's performance contributes very well to the overall group performance.

→ The student's reflection is of very good quality.

In line with expectations:

→ The performance demonstrates very good skill, poise and confidence.

→ The performance demonstrates very well the style/theme on which the final performance is based.

→ There is a reasonable level of creativity evident.

→ The student's performance contributes very well to the overall group performance.

→ The student's reflection is of good quality.

Yet to meet expectations:

→ The performance demonstrates a very basic level of skill, poise and confidence.

→ The performance does not contribute clearly to the style/theme on which the final performance is based.

→ The student's performance makes little contribution to the overall group performance.

→ The student's reflection is of limited quality.

CBA Reflection Form – Gymnastics

Consider using some of these words in your reflection:

Word Bank				
unison	canon	synchronisation	alignment	choreography
poise	transition	composition	sequence	tension
extension	flow	matching	mirroring	spotter
counterbalance	base	straddle	sudden	creativity
pathway				

1 **Which gymnastics themes did our performance demonstrate?**

Balance ☐   Transfer of weight ☐   Travel ☐

2 **I demonstrated poise (e.g. head position, hand action, extension, graceful movement) in my sequence when I …**

_____

_____

3 I demonstrated my range of skills (e.g. inversion, balances, solo/partner/ group, jumps, level of difficulty) when I successfully …

4 I demonstrated confidence (e.g. timing, skill technique, start, finish, landing, balance, solo) when I …

5 I demonstrated my creativity (e.g. use of transitions, space, time, flow, relationship, music or apparatus) when I …

6 My individual contribution to the performance (e.g. as base, top, lead, follower, choreographer, planner, video analyst, conditioning coach, participation, energy) was …

7 My overall feeling about my performance (not just a list or description; I recognise my strengths and room for improvement) is …

Reflection Review Checklist

● I named the theme/s on which the sequence is based (e.g. balance, transfer of weight, travel).	
● I identified points in the sequence where I demonstrate poise (e.g. head position, hand action, extension, graceful movement).	
● I identified points in the sequence where I demonstrate confidence (e.g. timing, skill technique, start, finish, landing).	
● I identified the range of skills I used (e.g. level of difficulty, inversion, balances, solo/partner/group, jumps, transitions).	
● I explained how my performance was creative (e.g. use of space, time, flow, relationship, music or apparatus).	
● I explained my individual contribution to the performance (e.g. as base, top, lead, follower, choreographer, planner, video analyst, conditioning coach, participation, energy).	
● My reflection is an honest judgement of my performance (not just a listing or description; I recognise my limitations and strengths).	
● I have used accurate gymnastics terms in my account.	

Signature: _____

Date: _____

Junior Cycle Profile of Achievement Statement

Composing your Junior Cycle Profile of Achievement Statement

At the end of the Junior Cycle you will be provided with an opportunity to recognise your learning in Physical Education on the **Junior Cycle Profile of Achievement**. You can include a statement on your most important learning and/or the results of your selected CBA. The material provided here will help you to compose that statement.

Step 1

Think about the various activities that have been highlighted for you in Physical Education during Junior Cycle. For example:

> I have surprised myself by completing a 0–5 k as part of my Physical Activity for Health and Wellbeing strand.

> I created a gymnastics performance with my classmates that lasted a full two minutes.

> I led an activity for my classmates – something that I was really dreading.

Step 2

Now think about how you demonstrated your learning as you were involved in those activities. Consider the key skills and wellbeing indicators as a guide. For example:

> I have surprised myself by completing a 0–5 k as part of my Physical Activity for Health and Wellbeing strand. In completing the 5 k I learned to draw up a training program and demonstrated my commitment and resilience in seeing it through.

> I created a gymnastics performance with my classmates that lasted a full two minutes. In completing the gymnastics performance, I learned to be creative and to do my best as part of a team at an activity I am not familiar with.

343

I led an activity for my classmates – something that I was really dreading. In leading the warm-up, I was aware of my nervousness. I learned some strategies and demonstrated my resilience.

Junior Cycle Profile of Achievement Statement in PE

20 [ ] [ ] –20 [ ] [ ]

What was your favourite moment of Junior Cycle Physical Education? Why?

My favourite moment of JCPE was when _____

_____

This was my favourite moment because _____

_____

What was your least favourite moment of Junior Cycle Physical Education? Why?

My least favourite moment of JCPE was when _____

_____

Which unit did you learn most about yourself in? What did you learn?

_____

_____

_____

The statement that I feel best represents my learning in PE at Junior Cycle is ...

_____

_____

_____

Signature: _____

Date: _____

Parent/Guardian Signature: _____

Date: _____